D0876864

George W. Bowman III

Dying, Grieving, Faith, and Family
A Pastoral Care Approach

More pre-publication
REVIEWS, COMMENTARIES, EVALUATIONS . . .

"**G**eorge Bowman has 'been there and felt that' of which he writes in this remarkably clear pastoral care approach to dying, grieving, faith, and family. His tent has been pitched close to the doorway of life's exit, and he has marked his journey for us to feel, embrace, and learn from his life-finding steps.

His skills as a C.P.E. supervisor, pastor, and counselor shine through to validate his directions for us. Caregivers and would-be caregivers will welcome this guide for the 'valley and shadow' days. Ministers will find this volume to be must reading in their search for the higher ground of life's faith-living."

J. Dewey Hobbs Jr., DMin
Former Director of the Department of Pastoral Care,
North Carolina Baptist Hospitals, Inc.,
Winston-Salem, North Carolina

"**T**he author's own life-threatening illnesses and years of counseling families in grief make this a book whose depths and resonance are invaluable and unique. Bowman unmasks the fear, anger, and pain of dying persons and their families in an unforgettable way. He manages to link family systems theory with the value of religious faith in offering pastoral care to the dying and the grieving. This book offers a hands-on approach for clergy, counselors, social workers, chaplains, and physicians in medical or hospice settings.

Bowman insists that one must face the grief episodes in one's own life before offering care to others. In doing so he changes pastoral care from stuffy professionalism to empathic concern. This is a very moving book, and does a marvelous job of enabling all readers to 'get inside' the experience of dying persons and their families."

Richard L. Morgan, PhD
Parish Associate,
Older Adult Ministries,
First Presbyterian Church;
Director of Pastoral Care,
Grace Healthcare Systems,
Morganton, North Carolina

The Haworth Pastoral Press
An Imprint of The Haworth Press, Inc.

Dying, Grieving, Faith, and Family

A Pastoral Care Approach

THE HAWORTH PASTORAL PRESS
Religion and Mental Health

Harold G. Koenig, MD,
Senior Editor

New, Recent, and Forthcoming Titles:

Adventures in Senior Living: Learning How to Make Retirement Meaningful and Enjoyable by J. Lawrence Driskill

Dying, Grieving, Faith, and Family: A Pastoral Care Approach by George W. Bowman

The Pastoral Care of Depression: A Guidebook by Binford W. Gilbert

Understanding Clergy Misconduct in Religious Systems: Scapegoating, Family Secrets, and the Abuse of Power by Candace R. Benyei

Dying, Grieving, Faith, and Family
A Pastoral Care Approach

George W. Bowman III

The Haworth Pastoral Press
An Imprint of The Haworth Press, Inc.
New York • London

Published by

The Haworth Pastoral Press, an imprint of The Haworth Press, Inc., 10 Alice Street, Binghamton, NY 13904-1580

Cover design by Marylouise E. Doyle.

Library of Congress Cataloging-in-Publication Data

Bowman, George W.
    Dying, grieving, faith, and family : a pastoral care approach / George W. Bowman III.
      p.   cm.
    Includes bibliographical references and index.
    ISBN 0-7890-0263-9 (alk. paper).
    1. Church work with the terminally ill. 2. Church work with the bereaved. 3. Church work with families. 4. Faith development. I. Title.
BV4460.6.B69 1997
259'.6—dc21   97-14091
                                                     CIP

To my wife, Betty, whose constant love, infinite patience, abounding cheerfulness, and inherent goodness continue to inspire me and help to keep hope alive in me and in others.

To Frances Wray and George W. Bowman Jr., my mother and father, whose most meaningful contribution to my life has been their visible and verbal communication to me that loving and caring are more important than anything else in life. My regret lies in my realization that during the preparation of this work both of them died and could not be a part of this harvest. I celebrate in faith their legacy to me, remember the lessons they taught me, and that both of them knew what it means to live fully and to die graciously.

To my many mentors, friends, colleagues, professional associates, and my dear children and stepchildren who forgave my mistakes, encouraged me, and always made me feel loved.

ABOUT THE AUTHOR

George W. Bowman III, ThM, recently retired from his position as Director of Hospital Ministry for the Department of Pastoral Care, North Carolina Baptist Hospitals, Inc. He is a Certified Chaplain Supervisor by the Association for Clinical Pastoral Education, a Fellow of the College of Chaplains of the American Protestant Hospital Association, and a Pastoral Affiliate for the American Association of Pastoral Counselors. Mr. Bowman is also a member of the Board of Directors for Hospice of North Carolina and Founding President of Hospice of Winston-Salem/Forsyth County. He has served as pastor at several Baptist churches in Virginia and three terms as Deacon of the Knollwood Baptist Church.

CONTENTS

Preface

It is altogether fair for one to raise the question, "Why another book on ministering to dying persons and grieving survivors?" For the writer it is important for two reasons.

First, for twenty years of parish ministry and more than thirty years of pastoral care to dying persons and grieving survivors at North Carolina Baptist Medical Center in Winston-Salem, my work has been concerned with understanding the processes, the losses, and the pains of these persons; of applying and integrating insights of behavioral sciences; and of wrestling with them in faith issues, and in seeking to help them make sense of their religious heritage and theological dilemmas as well as my own.

Second, the discovery that despite evolving processes occurring in one's development of a meaningful personal faith and the impacting influence of each person's family system and family of origin, little with which this author is familiar addresses how faith and family systems figure into management, coping, resolving, or recovery when dying and grieving become a part of our life's experiences.

Ministries to the dying and grieving have largely been approached more or less in individualistic ways. This can be easily justified and is often the only recourse. I contend that fruitful and profound results are realized when one takes into account the person's and the family's faith journey and the life experiences of one's family system. In attempting such a venture the author is aware of the dangers of incompleteness, of oversimplification, of biases, and of subjectivism. This work, therefore, is an attempt to be descriptive, suggestive, provocative, and invitational with respect to urging the reader to explore more deeply faith, moral development, and family systems theory and practice. Hopefully the thoughts, feelings, and ideas expressed here will stimulate further study and practice by the reader.

The pastor seeking to minister to the hurts and concerns of troubled persons soon realizes that one never reaches that place of expertise which precludes new ideas and new discoveries. The first thirty or so years of my experience was marked by more questions than answers. Much of what we learn is gained through our own experiences of failures and successes.

Some twenty to twenty-five years ago a number of us experienced significant learnings from mentors in the field of dying and death, among whom were the renowned pioneers, Dr. Elisabeth Kübler-Ross, practitioner and author, and Dr. Cecily Saunders, a creator and teacher in the modern hospice movement. Most pastors were introduced to grief through the works of Erich Lindemann and Edgar Jackson, among others. We stand in their debt. It is generally agreed that work done in dying and death in the intervening decades has been one of study, modification, refinement, and correction of those who helped us to make discussions of dying and death less taboo and more honorable, as well as to inspire more courageous efforts in caring for persons. Without a doubt, significant contributions have been made since that time, but by and large the work done has been built upon the foundations which they established. Occasionally there does come another significant work that helps to amplify, concretize, and integrate our knowledge of these concerns. Hardly anyone can attempt such a task without recourse to some of the basic approaches made by those pioneers. Perhaps it is only our own commitment to productive ways of utilizing the legacy of others that gives credibility to our own search. It is in the utilization and implementation of received knowledge that one comes to discover further knowledge for oneself.

Initially, my experience inclined me to work with the stage idea of dying and the process dynamics of grief. After a few years I discovered something that doubtless had been pointed out but had been neglected, namely, that family members also experience a lot of the same processes; some years after I discovered that those of the helping teams of physicians, nurses, social workers, and clergy were caught up in quite the same emotional, mental, and spiritual experiences as the dying and the grieving. In looking more seriously at faith, moral development, and experiences with family systems, it became clear that more significant ministry occurs when we are guided by insights as to how faith develops and how family systems impact these persons in the crises of dying and grieving.

Faith development and family systems theory are both far more comprehensive than can be summed up in a work of this kind. It is my intention to set forth precepts and ideas that can be useful to the pastor in his ministry to dying persons and grieving survivors. In being true to this purpose, comprehensive and complete presentations are not attempted, and critiques are avoided. I make sincere efforts to represent these theorists fairly and hope to present an accurate understanding of their significant contributions. Should this at least partially be realized, this author will be satisfied. Understanding both family systems theory and moral/faith development affords significant help as we seek to apply these in our ministries to dying persons and grieving survivors.

"Experience is the best teacher" is an adage that is common currency for most persons. Those involved in face-to-face, hands-on ministry to dying persons and their families are aware of the importance of another adage: "Dying persons and their survivors are our best teachers" of ministry to these persons. An additional "best" teacher is one's own personal experience with terminal illness and grief. It is important for the minister to be open to his own experience with life-threatening illnesses and grief. Having learned from a number of mentors and educators, my own experience with two life-threatening illnesses—cancer and spinal meningitis—provided valuable insights for ministry to dying and grieving persons.

In 1976, I was diagnosed as having cancer of the colon. When my physician, Dr. Wallace Wu, said to me, "Chaplain Bowman, you have cancer," I was emotionally terrified and intellectually shaken. A colon resection was performed by Dr. Timothy Pennell. I ran the gamut of feelings and thoughts—bodily pain and spiritual anguish. I was forced to face the possibility of my own death. I, the pastor who had helped so many others walk that lonely and forbidding road to death, now had to face it myself. Although the physician's diagnosis of my cancer was not welcomed into my life, it enabled me to confront, grasp, and understand many of the physical, mental, emotional, and spiritual dynamics and concerns previously witnessed and experienced with other persons: shock, denial, anger, fears, embarrassment, guilt, bargaining, acceptance, and other responses addressed later in this work.

Four years later, it became my misfortune to be infected with a deadly bacteria, pseudomonas, which by virtue of a lesion found its way into my spinal fluid and rendered me blind for several weeks. Thanks to skilled physicians, Dr. Robert Kohut and Dr. Eben Alexander, two powerful antibiotics, skilled medical and nursing care, and support of family and Christian community, the abscess was removed and my life was saved. Medical knowledge at that time indicated little or no chance for my survival. The prognosis was that I would die, or be left permanently blind, or if I recovered my sight, severe damage would leave me mindless and incompetent to think. It became clear after full recovery from both cancer and spinal meningitis—one terminal and the other catastrophic—that death can come over a period of time or instantaneously. Life-threatening illnesses bring soberness of thought, awareness of life's fragility, and the necessity to face the reality of death.

In profound ways these illnesses have contributed to awarenesses that seldom come any other way and have provided an opportunity for exploring the nature and power of physical, emotional, mental, and spiritual resources. Significant strength comes from possessing the will to live and a competitive spirit; mental acuity and resiliency; emotional insights and freedom of emotional expression; and a personal faith in God profoundly experienced and visibly supported by one's religious community and church. For me there are no substitutes.

Success in dealing with my profound pains can be attributed to using the vibrant resources and support systems available to me. These included my own personal faith in God, my belief in the goodness of life, my life-long will to live, my competitive spirit, my sense of humor, and my willingness to become dependent. No less important to me were my wife, Betty; my children Karen, Greg, Chris, Holly, and Bryan; my mother, Frances; my siblings Charlotte, Virginia, and Jon; their spouses Cameron and Penny; my extended family; colleagues of brothers and sisters in the Department of Pastoral Care, Maurice Briggs, Mac Wallace, Ken Burnette, Pat Garrett, L. L. McGee, Andy Lester, Ted Dougherty, Mahan Siler, Wesley Brett, Charles Wilson, Dewey Hobbs, Swan Haworth, Sharon Engebretson, Jane Litzinger, Mark Jensen, John Edgerton, Jay Foster, Neil Chafin, Mary Catherine Hasty, Joseph Mulligan, Bob Spillman, James Hyde, and Everett Thomas; the Pastoral Care support staff of Barbara Matthews, Shirley Hasty, Karen Kimbrell, Bertie Slate, and Carolyn Kite; my church fellowship of Knollwood Baptist Church with its pastoral staff of Jack Noffsinger, John Totten, Kirk Neely, Steve Meriwether, Tom Austin, and their spouses; scores of Clinical Pastoral Education (CPE) students and residents; untold number of colleagues in the Mid-Atlantic Region of Association of Clinical Pastoral Education, the College of Chaplains, Inc., Association of Clinical Pastoral Education, and American Association of Pastoral Counseling; many friends in the larger community of Winston-Salem, friends statewide and nationally in Hospice; and my daily readings of the Psalms and Book of Common Prayer. All of these individuals and support systems taught me what patients, families, colleagues, and friends experience when dying and when death abruptly or casually arrests our lives. Many persons have been my teachers and mentors. For those who have pioneered my own efforts, I give thanks. In those places from the vast literature where credit has not been given, I offer my apologies.

It is out of these experiences that this work is authenticated. It is out of these experiences that my spirit and mind are motivated to attempt this task. For sake of convenience the masculine gender is employed. This in no way reflects bias by the author, but rather that employment of her/his, she/he becomes cumbersome. I am incontrovertibly and irrevocably committed to erasing those unjust distinctions in gender that we have tolerated and perpetuated too long. I ask the reader to substitute pronominal designations as desired.

I recognize my omission of a more exhaustive and more thorough work on pastoral care to children and to AIDS patients/families. I confess to a measure of ineptness and lack of experience in pastoral caregiving to dying children/parents/siblings. This omission is doubtless egregious. It would also be assumptive to attempt to deal with this important ministry casually and irresponsibly. The reader is encouraged to read those works in the bibliography for more information.

Information on AIDS and its related infectious states changes daily, instanced by recent drug discoveries for amelioration of symptomatology and possible cure. Projections of number of persons infected, those diagnosed with full-blown AIDS, hospitalization costs, infection controls, treatment plans, promise of cure, drug effectiveness, and epidemiology become revised almost hourly. Ministers are compelled to stay informed for meaningful pastoral care to be compassionate, intelligent, and productive.

Appreciation is expressed to Sharon Doar for helping me to understand and conceptualize faith development, and to Barbara Sale for her consummate patience and skills in preparing these materials.

Chapter 1

Faith Development in the Crises of Dying and Grieving

The individual's and family's management of emotions, mental anguish, and spiritual concerns is profoundly influenced by religious beliefs and faith systems to which these persons have been committed and by which they live. No crisis brings these into focus more clearly than with the dying and grieving. Along with the development of personality comes development of morality and faith. In moral and faith development Freud, Piaget, Kohlberg (1976), Fowler (1982, 1984), and more recently Gilligan (1982), Belenky et al. (1986) have contributed to our understandings. Following the earlier work of Freud and Piaget, attention in recent years has focused on the work of Kohlberg and Fowler.[1] Gilligan and colleagues[2] have observed that earlier work begun by Freud and Piaget was largely based upon male perceptions of moral development and these authors have appropriately suggested that men and women approach moral decisions from different perspectives. Men and women commonly do not approach epistemology or ways of knowing and thinking in the same way. They contend that males reach decisions differently from females in the consideration of moral and/or religious dilemmas and issues. Their insights indicate how strongly male and female individual and family systems issues lend themselves to conflicts in grief-producing crises. Further understanding of the complicity of each family's difficulty in stress management, triangling, escalation, polarization, and stasis in family systems theory must not be ignored. It is necessary for pastors to keep these processes in mind as they seek to give aid. The sensitive, astute, and thoughtful pastor/theologian will take seriously the ways in which faith development takes shape and how it works for persons and families in crisis.

Fruitful dialogue about moral development, ways of knowing (Belenky et al., 1986), religious/spiritual decision making, and differences in ways of knowing have sought to take seriously earlier contributions by Freud and Piaget, modified and extended by Kohlberg, Fowler, and others. Sigmund Freud observed and contended (from his biological bias) that humans are unsocialized and amoral. He held to the idea that persons develop morally out of the interplay between the social and instinctual (as conceived largely of unconscious desires).[3]

In his way of understanding human personality development Freud posited the concepts of superego, ego or ego ideal, and id or impulse. The child develops in his moral (or spiritual) growth by seeking to make sense out of the demands of society (or family) and the strongly experienced inner impulses and desires for self-gratification. For him the external demand or superego wages war with the developing child's growing need for gratification of the id. The heavy constraints of external forces and influences give rise to hostility and aggressiveness. The developing ego (and ego ideal) serves the child as the mediator between the external influences and the internal desires. Morals and morality were understood as being repressive and constraining. For balance to be maintained by the anxiety-ridden child, defenses or ways of coping are developed partially through resistance and partially through introjection of social influences which lead to a developing sense of personal morals.[4] Social realities being what they are, his mechanistic assessment is neither satisfying nor accurate. It is believed by many that the religious/spiritual nature of humans resists the notion that religious values can be written off as restrictive and oppressive as opposed to these values serving as stabilizing resources.

Piaget was more positive about humans, humanness, and the human condition. He contended that moral principles become developed as society and the individual interrelate; as children interact with adult authority persons. In these transactions involving rightness/wrongness the child decides upon morals in the context of fairness and justice—what is right for me and others; what is wrong for me and others; is right or wrong for both when both I and they are fair and just. Logic and reasoning are important. As the child grows in knowledge of the consequences of moral action, more sophisticated reasoning occurs. Piaget has shown that morals, rules, and principles in moral development parallel cognitive development. Reason and reasoning take shape as cognitive capacities develop. Physical, mental, and emotional growth and development occur in somewhat predictable ways as the child's self interfaces with and relates to other selves in psychological and moral development and growth. The child moves from the centristic self to the heteronomous self (regard for others and self), and forward to the stage of the autonomous self. Cognition and reasoning proceed along the lines of the developing psychological self.

Lawrence Kohlberg has taken what appears to be the essential nugget of the pioneer work of Piaget and developed it along a design of cognitive development.[5] In the process he has sought to refine some of the work of Piaget and to give clearer perspective. While elaborated upon slightly different lines by others (and therefore modified to some extent), he does not radically depart from Piaget. While at once and the same time remaining true to the essential nugget, he does elucidate the implications, design, and force of the developing child's psychological and moral development. There is little observable substantial change in his thrust, since he does argue cogently for Piaget's case. One of the difficulties of the theories of both Piaget and Kohlberg has been pointed out, namely, they do not take seriously the importance of a developing self. My primary criticism lies in their refusal or reluctance to take seriously spiritual development, religious experiences of early years and into adolescence, the positive or negative influences in superego development, and the varied stimuli in the person's religious mileau. It is difficult to imagine that the developing child psychologically is bereft of certain spiritual influences. Varying as they may be, these influences are nevertheless important. In Kohlberg's moral stages and moralization—the cognitive development approach—he is wedded to a linear development. He contends that there are three major developmental stages of reasoning: the intuitive, the concrete operational, and the formal operational.

At around the age of seven the child enters the stage of concrete logical thought; he can then make logical inferences, classify things, and handle quantitative relations about concrete things.[6]

In adolescence, many, but not all individuals enter this stage of formal operations, at which level they can reason abstractly.

Kohlberg (1976) is correct in observing that "almost no adolescents and adults will still be entirely at the stage of concrete operation, many will be at the stage of partial formal operations, and most will be the highest stage of formal operations."[7] The weakness of such argument lies in the avoidance of taking seriously external stimulation and societal experiences constantly experienced as well as the constitutional and hereditary possessions of individuals and their variants. Add to this, as a number of friendly critics have observed[8] (Gilligan, Belenky, Clinchy, Goldberger, Tarule, Brownfield, and others), the subjects of research and investigation have been males, not females. Certain spiritual and religious influences present in the developing child at least have the possibility of skewing research into different directions despite attempts to the contrary. It is impossible to dismiss out of hand Kohlberg's work and conclusions.

But what is his schema, what is his approach, and wherein lies the value of his research and endeavors? Since the primary purpose of this study is to seek to make application of moral, spiritual, and faith development, as well as integration, to minister to the dying person and survivors, it is impossible to do more than a brief summary. He proposes the six moral stages of three specific levels: Level One—preconventional, Level Two—conventional, and Level Three—postconventional or principled.[9] In each of his three levels he suggests two stages.

Level One is *preconventional* and is designed in stage one, heteronomous morality, and stage two, individualism, instrumental purpose, and exchange. With heteronomous morality, there is an avoidance of breaking of rules, backed by punishment, and obedience for one's own sake with the emphasis upon avoiding physical damage to persons and property. The reasons for doing right are the avoidance of punishment and the superior power of authorities. Resulting is confusion of authorities' perspective with one's own perspective. Conflict arises between authorities' rules and principles with one's own feelings and personal development.

At the preconventional level, stage two, one follows rules when one gains something from the transaction and consequent decision.

One acts to meet one's own interest and needs while at the same time lets others do the same. Right is fair, wrong is unfair, when there is equal exchange as a deal made or when agreement is reached. One's reasons for doing right come out of one's awareness that one serves one's own needs or interests in a world where there is recognition that other persons have rights and interests. Also, when one's self-growth and psychological development occurs, the *conventional level* (Level Two), the self moves in moral development to stage three.

In stage three mutual interpersonal expectations, relationships, and interpersonal conformity begin to become incorporated. What is right consists of one's living up to what is expected by people who are close, or what people generally expect of persons in one's role as son, brother, or friend. *Being good* is important and means having good motives, showing concern for others, and keeping mutual relationships of trust, loyalty, respect, and gratitude. One begins to care for others. There comes a belief in the golden rule—do unto others as you would have others do unto you—and an authority which supports what is understood as good behavior.

With Kohlberg, stage four in the conventional level of moral development and behavior the person develops the awareness that society is larger than one's own self. Social systems and the individualized conscience come into play. One then begins to fulfill the actual duties to which one has agreed. Right becomes a matter of contributing to society, to the group, or to the institution. Reasons for doing right undergo more sophisticated change and modification. As one seeks to maintain balance and to keep the institution or society or community functioning well as a whole, one comes to have respect for rules and authority, belief in these rules and authority, as well as a willingness to abide by these. As a developing person comes to Level Three, the *postconventional* or *principled level*, still further development, beliefs, codes of conduct, and values become important and normative. Social contract (or utility) and individual rights are formed and followed.

With stage five comes the awareness that persons hold a variety of values and opinions. Values and rules are consistent with one's own group. These values and rules are stated, upheld, and enforced in the interest and welfare of the group without partiality. With these values and rules come expectations and social obligations. When these values and rules do not prevail, chaos results and persons do not achieve or maintain levels of desired development and maturity. These relative rules should usually be upheld, however, in the interest of impartiality and because they are social contracts or covenants implied as a means of avoiding chaos, anarchy, and nonproductive results. Kohlberg holds that some nonrelative values and rights—such as life and liberty—must be upheld in any society regardless of majority opinion. Moral development thus attained inclines one toward respect for others, sometimes to the neglect of one's own individual desires, proclivities, opinions, and impulses. (When society itself or the larger community subscribes to such values and behavior, the autistic or narcissistic person obviously is controlled by the larger social group.) With this fifth stage of postconventional or principled development a sense of obligation to law develops because of one's social contract to make and abide by laws for the welfare of all and for the protection of the rights of all. This conviction ensures that the person has come to value the validity of universal moral principles and has a sense of personal commitment to them. The person is agreeable to consensual norms and principles for that society. The individual in his respect for society's values then owns these values for the greater good for the greater number of persons. Cognitive development awareness is actualized.

In reaching stage six, universal ethical principles within the context of postconventional or principled moral development, the individual becomes aware that people hold a variety of values and opinions, and that most values and rules are relative to the group of which one is a part. These relative rules are to be upheld in the interest of impartiality; they are a part of the social contract. As one reaches this stage of universal ethical principles one then moves from the emphasis upon the social contract to that plateau of self-chosen ethical principles.

Particular laws or social agreements are valid and rest upon such principles. These principles are mindful of the acquiescence of the individual as one submits to more universal principles, the greatest good for all persons. Principles of justice, equality in human rights, respect for the dignity of humans as individual persons, and commitment to the endeavor of making these universal principles of right and wrong for all persons as the norm for development and consequent behavior are espoused and followed. One becomes committed to the idea of what is good for all is good for one.

The sense of obligation to law because of one's social responsibility in the social contract to making and abiding by laws for the welfare of all characterizes beliefs and behavior. The rationally developed person holds that universal moral principles are written into the fabric of being in such ways that personal commitment to and observance of these universal moral principles makes for a more wholesome environment. It also makes for a more rational approach to conflictual dilemmas presented in life and a viewpoint or perspective that persons themselves are valuable and should be regarded as such. Liberty and justice for all becomes the desired norm. The freedom to be one's own person within the context of social obligations which do not transgress the rights, the parameters of justice, and regard for the intrinsic value of another becomes the desired, mature stage of moral (spiritual/religious) welfare for all.

James Fowler (1984) receives primary credit for understanding of faith development along specifically Christian lines. His faith development construct utilizes Erikson's understanding of personality development. It is he who takes faith development by recourse to religious and Christian beliefs. His work, *Becoming Adult, Becoming Christian*, recapitulates his earlier faith development ideas.[10] He understands faith development to move through seven "stages of faith."[11]

PRIMAL FAITH (INCORPORATIVE SELF)

Primal faith is that faith of the infant characterized by trust and dependence upon those dependable realities of primary caregivers. These caregivers are experienced by the infant as beings of superordinate power and wisdom upon which the infant can safely depend. This particular stage of faith development, as Fowler suggests, correlates closely with Erikson's stage of trust versus mistrust. In the interrelationship of the parent/caretaker the infant learns what and who can be trusted and who can be trusted in the mutuality of interrelating.

INTUITIVE-PROJECTIVE FAITH
(IMPULSIVE SELF)

Intuitive-projective faith development begins to occur somewhere around age two when language, conversation, and verbal dialogue open new avenues of learning in both psychological and moral development. Fowler holds that the growing child has more mobility, more experiences, more perceptions, and more feelings which collaborate to mediate relations to the world and others in new and different ways. Out of the attention (and love or lack of it) which the child experiences, self-consciousness and self-centeredness emerge and temporarily solidify as the child comes to believe himself or herself to be the center of the world. This stage correlates Kohlberg's preconventional, centristic state in moral development. Fowler suggests that an awakening to reality occurs beyond everyday experiences as a child begins to differentiate the self from other selves. As permissions on the one hand and prohibitions on the other become a part of the child's reality framework, primitive ideas of right and wrong are beginning to emerge as well as a superprojected image(s) of God or gods. Good/evil, right/wrong, God/Devil, acceptable/nonacceptable, experiences and realities are part of the child's everyday life. Primary understandings and rituals become the experience of the growing child, and last up to and including the preschool years.

MYTHIC-LITERAL FAITH (IMPERIAL SELF)

Mythic-literal faith takes the child into the stage of a strong sense of belonging and being valued and cherished as a person. The need for affiliation with family and others becomes distinctive. The self is differentiated from others and yet senses a need to be valued by others and to belong. The changing of oneself is recognizable in relationship to family and group. Not only is the self important but the larger world of other selves becomes important.

It also means that in their thinking about right and wrong, good and evil, they can develop a strong sense of fairness based on reciprocity (and to paraphrase this means taking seriously rewards and punishments for doing good or doing evil, which becomes elevated to the level of the larger cosmic principle). Faith becomes a matter of reliance on the stories, rules, and implicit values of the family's community of meanings. Where the family (or its substitute) is related to a larger community of shared traditions and meanings, faith involves valuing the stories, practices and beliefs of that tradition. *Narrative* or story is the important idea here. Knowing the stories of "our people" becomes an important index of identification and of evaluation of self and others and their groups.[12]

Religious symbolism, ritual, and making distinctions between fact and fantasy is a part of the growing child's tasks and achievements. The mythic-literal phase or stage involves one in a growing awareness and strong sense of fairness (to use the categories of Piaget and Kohlberg justice). Right and wrong, rules and regulations, the embracing of values as oftentimes enshrined in rituals are a part of this developing stage and one in which the child moves into the period of adolescence.

SYNTHETIC-CONVENTIONAL FAITH (INTERPERSONAL SELF)

The developing person begins to emerge into early adolescence, Fowler contends, and those familiar with developmental psychology recognize that it corresponds to those tasks in early, mid, and late adolescence, through which experiential and experimental tasks one comes to a more comfortably solidified identity. This appears in late adolescence and early adulthood. Not only is there psychological but moral and religious growth involving a synthesizing and a concretizing. The person becomes more able to decipher the codes of reality with respect to one's own relating to reality. Exploration, experimentation, consolidation, and the beginning struggles to embrace adult structures occur. Life itself is experienced in more realistic decision making with respect to heterosexual development, the choosing of a vocation, the choice of educational pursuits, the choice of a mate, and the development of values, beliefs, and lifestyles. Fowler contends the following:

> The key to our understanding the structure and dynamics of this stage is an appreciation for a revolution that adolescence typically brings in cognitive development. No longer is it limited to the mental manipulation of concrete objects or representations and of observable processes. Now thinking begins to construct all sorts of ideal possibilities and hypothetical considerations.[13]

It is during this stage of psychological development that one's own personal identity comes to be more concretely experienced and formed. Involved are commitments of various sorts, the expression of one's own selfhood, and the beginnings of stronger, more viable differentiation from other identity-selves. Typically there is resistance to constructs, ideals, and expectations of other important persons. The testing grounds become those of ferment and rebelliousness. The person is involved in psychological and moral reasoning in a process of autonomy formation, which by nature develops along the lines of one's own synthesizing abilities, rather than the received or the given expectations of other persons, important as these may be. It is the exciting stage of becoming oneself. The process is one of putting together and synthesizing the variety of both consistent and disparate elements of one's experience with the family, the group, and humankind. This is the common experience of the self and selves which both incorporates and resists reality forces.

Crucial to the forming of the synthetic-conventional stage is the drawing together of one's own stories, values, and beliefs into a supportive and orienting unity.[14] One does not embrace the values and beliefs of others simply by precept or example but finds it necessary to explore, to examine, to critique, and to incorporate into oneself those components of experience which make sense to the individual and which appear to be consistent with those experiences. Those ideas and principles which do not add up are often discarded as valueless, irrelevant, or without practical benefit.

INDIVIDUATIVE-REFLECTIVE FAITH
(INSTITUTIONAL SELF)

When the person moves from the synthetic-conventional stage of moral and faith development certain avenues in decision making have been examined and explored, yet not so clearly solidified as to make it easy to make a clear-cut commitment. This adult stage involves one in further exploration of reality, objectifying one's relationship to reality, clearer self-determination, and self-differentiation. The self faces the enterprise of more clearly determining faith, faith stances, and faith redefinition—that which was comfortable and reassuring at earlier stages of development ceases to become as comfortable and satisfying. Personal autonomy becomes clearer, one's selfhood more important.

Biological growth and psychological development help to ensure the conviction that the self is an important person in one's own right to the degree that the developing faith becomes more assured and more self-affirming. Whatever faith has thus far developed necessarily becomes suspect to the point that it is reevaluated and reaffirmed along the lines of one's own self-expectations rather than the received faith of earlier stages, though these be enshrined in ritual and in the story of one's own experience. The boundaries of the self are more defined. Identity has become more consolidated. Beliefs and values are more clearly asserted and more firmly held.

As one comes into a more authentic selfhood, more self-assurance results. The authentic person owns and bears deeply held convictions, beliefs, and values. Emerging is a stronger sense of responsibility and accountability to others and to one's self. As Fowler indicates by "individuative-reflective," the individual as she or he develops is faced with action, reflection, and action coming out of either failure or success. It is no longer comfortable for the person to simply receive without question: it is necessary for the individual to face the moral/religious dilemmas presented by life and its realities and to come to some cogency of faith commitment and some implementation of behavior that arises out of these convictions, beliefs, and values. Authenticity is important; also important is congruence between identity and outlook, selfhood and commitment, belief and action. It is important that one live by what one believes.

CONJUNCTIVE FAITH (INTERINDIVIDUAL SELF)

This adult stage involves one in a need to make sense of the myriad of one's experiences. What one believes and holds must stand up and be consistent in the crucible of experience. One has to square one's better self with one's worst self. With this comes the recognition that there is the dark, shadow side of the self which needs to be embraced and befriended. The realization that truth is complex, manifests itself in a variety of forms, and that few decisions are black/white, either/or, is discovered and implemented. One then becomes more open to a wider range of reality and life than one's own experiences, traditions, life stories, or limited vision. Fowler stated:

> By this time one has begun to have to deal with a new sense of the reality and power of death. Peers and some who are younger have died. Perhaps parents, and certainly many of their generation, have died. One recognizes that he/she may have lived more than half of an expectable lifetime, and the unmistakable signs of irreversible aging are both felt and visible.[15]

Hallmarks of the transition to conjunctive faith include the following: an awareness of the need to face and hold together several unmistakable polar tensions in one's life,[16] and to paraphrase, the polarities of being both old and young and of being both masculine and feminine. The polarity exists between that which is consciously felt and known as well as that which is unconsciously/consciously felt and known.

Life is seen and known not simplistically but as possessing definite complex elements, ambiguities, and incongruities. By this time in life one has been confronted with a maze of conflicted valences. One has come to discover that the world is larger than one's own community, family, state, nation, or world. Simple faith is no longer so simple. One comes to see that earlier learnings which have functioned rather well no longer can hold the key to unlocking all behavior we experience. One has to be willing to open oneself to other understandings of reality, truth, belief, values, traditions, and methods for making sense of the complexity of life, the world, human eccentricities and failures. One particular approach does not suffice to meet the demands thrust upon one by the real world. One then faces the mystifying and perplexing reality that it is impossible to deal with reality in provincial ways of thinking, feeling, or reasoning.

Conjunctive faith combines deep, particular commitments with principled openness to the truths of other traditions. It combines loyalty to one's own primary communities of value and belief with loyalty to the reality of a community of communities.[17]

Thus one's allegiance to what makes sense in one's own devoutly held faith is of importance and normative for that person. One recognizes that openness to other possibility does exist and invites the growing person of faith to explore these possibilities These possibilities contribute to one's own maturing faith, and are serviceable to one's own further moral and spiritual development.

UNIVERSALIZING FAITH (THEONOMY; OR AS I SUGGEST, THEONOMOUS)

The term "universalizing" may be bothersome as a gerundive; however, adjectivally it is descriptive of a continuing process, therefore useful.

Universalizing faith, in its authentic form, is recognizable in any culture or tradition. Despite differences in the metaphysical convictions and images were used to express them and despite differences in their understandings of the relation of being in time, the quality of the lives of persons of Universalizing Faith from whatever time or tradition are demonstrably similar in spirit and power.[18]

Decentralization of the self is necessary to the process of universalizing. It is noteworthy that there is movement from the first of Fowler's stages, the Primal Stage, in which the person has sensed one's self as the center of human existence, and attention is given to the decentralized self in the Universalizing stage. The process becomes one of continuing to include other reality data. Wider religious ideas are befriended and embraced. In the stage of maturing faith there is both a qualitative and quantitative expansion in perspective and outlook.

Universalizing faith goes beyond previous stages to include the possibility that other faith systems have validity. The incorporation of other faith viewpoints broadens and enriches the person's own faith. The faith development perspective (of Universalizing faith) depends on the conviction . . . "that each person or community continually experience the availability of Spirit and its powerful transformation."[19]

> The goal . . . is not for everyone to reach the stage of Universalizing faith. Rather, it is for each person or group to open themselves, as radically as possible—within the structures of the present stage or transition—to synergy with Spirit. The dynamics of that openness—and the extraordinary openness that comes occasionally with "saving Grace"—operate as lure and power toward ongoing faith in partnership with Spirit and in the direction of Universalizing faith.[20]

Fowler's faith development approach from a distinctively Christian viewpoint (despite his critics) does provide useful understandings and insights for the pastor. Since the pastoral care practitioner ministers to dying and grieving persons from a faith perspective, Fowler's work is informative and suggestive. In his chapter, "Faith and the Structuring of Meaning," Fowler maintains that faith is relational as well as results from knowing. "Faith begins in a relationship. Faith implies trust in another, reliance upon another, a counting upon or dependence upon another." Also, "Faith is a way of being, arising out of a way of *seeing* and *knowing*," therefore is a knowing.[21] He suggests a summary of his understanding of faith as:

> The process of constitutive-knowledge

> Underlying a person's composition and maintenance of a comprehensive frame (or frames) of meaning

> Generated from the person's attachments or commitments to centers of supraordinate value which have power to unify his or her experiences of the world

> Thereby endowing the relationships, contexts, and patterns of everyday life, past and future, with significance[22]

He takes more seriously the self and ego development than do his predecessors. He contends "that the constitutive-knowing by which self-other relationships are constituted does not involve just an extension of the logic of rational certainty." He suggests that ". . . faith is a core processing the total self-constitutive activity that is ego."[23] Ego and ego development become the integrative centers around which faith clusters.

Fowler's work has provoked lively and creative discussion and dialogue. Craig Dykstra (1986) claims to have culled through what he believes to be the "essential ingredients" from Fowler's writings. In "What Is Faith? An Experiment in the Hypothetical Mode," he states that faith according to Fowler has the following central features.[24]

1. Faith is a human activity (not a thing people have, but a way of knowing and being which they are engaged in.
2. Faith is an activity that takes place through relationships.
3. The most significant aspects of these relationships are the aspects of trust and loyalty.
4. Faith involves some object(s). In faith we trust in and are loyal to something.
5. In faith we are related in trust and loyalty not only to persons and groups, but also to the "supraordinate centers of value and power, i.e., the "gods" to which the people in groups whom we trust and are loyal to are also related.
6. Through these relationships of trust and loyalty, our "world" (both proximate and ultimate) is shaped, meaning is made, and our own selves are constituted.
7. This activity of world-shaping, meaning-making, or "constitutive knowing" is the core activity which defines faith.

As logical correlatives to this understanding of *faith* and "faith development" it follows that faith is a human universal and thus it is impossible for humans to live in a world without some sort of meaning and some sense of self. Faith continually undergoes change (which Fowler himself claims since faith development does not move back and forth between one stage or another). Faith development does not carry the expectation that one grows and matures step by step or stage by stage. His contention safeguards against conceiving faith as a building-block process of stacking one stage on top of another in order to erect the most desired and optimal edifice.

Dykstra is correct in his appraisal that Fowler's strong Christian orientation makes it impossible for him to give much credence to other faiths. This contention could be challenged in that Fowler at least hints at this in his universalizing stage. Nevertheless, he appears to back away from being more than suggestive of the value of other religious faiths. Dykstra finds himself more in the company of John Cobb ("Christ in a Pluralistic Age"). Both Cobb and Dykstra correlate faith with the divine. With Dykstra ". . . faith is appropriate and intentional participation in the redemptive activity of God."[25] Faith then becomes a way of relating to what is, not just what is taken to be, and finds reality to be that which ". . . is the ultimate source of meaning and the ground of all existence." He feels by such definition and understanding that faith is not necessarily a human universal. He proposes that faith is a possibility but not a necessity as such; it is an activity of response to who God is and what God is doing; and that faith so understood requires particular kinds of knowledge. One needs to know who God is and what God is doing in order to respond. While not stated as such, it does involve certain developing influences which come into the life of the *believer* and *knower.* Learning the appropriate response to God's redeeming activity involves knowing something about ourselves and necessitates awarenesses of a developing self and a personhood.

One's faith, moral development, worldview, and belief system cannot be avoided by the pastor in dealing meaningfully with dying and grieving persons. It is important for the caregiver to be open to those faith systems that surface. Clarity about one's own faith and spiritual formation is important also. It is for this purpose that moral and faith development issues have been thus summarized. It is important to recognize that to be an effective pastor one does not necessarily need to become involved in the intricacies, refinements, and critiques of faith development. Faith and moral development cannot be regarded as something simplistically received, but vital to wholesome adjustment and taken into account in the pastor's ministry to dying persons and grieving survivors.

GENDER DIFFERENCES:
CAROL GILLIGAN AND FEMININE VOICES

It has been contended by Gilligan, Belenky and her colleagues, and others that faith development research, investigations, and posited theories have either not taken seriously or disregarded women in their psychological, emotional, and spiritual/moral development. Such has been the case with Freud, Piaget, and to some extent, Kohlberg. This is not altogether true of Fowler; he at least acknowledges some differences. The importance of "women's ways of knowing" (Belenky et al., 1986) and the "different voice" (Gilligan, 1982) focus an emphasis readily recognized by the pastor in the family's dynamic responses and reactions, and in ways of seeking to resolve the oftentimes complicated issues that surface with dying persons and grieving survivors. These differences in masculine/feminine faith development in family relationships are not to be ignored in pastoral ministry. In Langdale's (Supp, 1986) "A Re-Vision of Structural-Development Theory," she suggests the following:

> *Moral orientation and gender.* Traditional structural-development theory has not entertained the question of gender differences. Yet gender, like the concept of morality itself, is a universal characteristic of human experience. People are both either male or female, and the male/female dichotomy, however problematical, exists and has existed in every culture.
>
> As a universal characteristic of human experience, gender is a psychological category of difference, central to people's interpretation of their own experiences in large part because children become aware of their own identity as females and males very early in the life cycle (by the age of three), and because this aspect of their identity remains with them throughout the life cycle.[27]

Gilligan states that developmental psychology has been unclear and has ignored the developmental differences in males and females. In the writings of Freud and Piaget (and largely Erikson, English, and Pearson) women have been treated as though they were men. Males have been the sample in the construction of developmental theories.

Over the past ten years I have been listening to people talking about morality and about themselves. Half way through that time, I began to hear a distinction in these voices, two ways of speaking about moral problems, two modes of describing the relationship between other and self.[28]

Gilligan's observations launched her into critical research resulting in a "clearer representation of women's development" and in which study she sets forth distinctive differences in approaching moral development with women. I agree that earlier developmental theories have ignored female development. Culture has dictated (quite wrongly) that women think like men, act like men, and follow male psychological and moral development along the same lines or patterns. Women, "having been kept in their place," have largely been perceived as deferring to the male in matters of judgment. (If disputes, conflicts, disagreements over territorial and national boundaries, and the complexities of international relationships were left to women in a world in which men had little to say about such issues, perhaps there would be fewer wars, murders, killings, and national and international unrest.)

Gilligan does not argue that the female experience, growth, and moral development is necessarily better than the male developmental viewpoint, only that it is distinctly different in significant respects. Both male and female are concerned about responsibility. The focus for women, however, is upon compassion and care while with men it is upon rights and justice. For women ". . . identity is defined in the context of relationship and judged by a standard of responsibility and care. . . . Morality is seen . . . as arising from the experience of connection and conceived as a problem of inclusion rather than one of balancing claims."[29]

"For . . . men, the tone of identity is different, clearer, more direct, more distinct, and sharp-edged,"[30] which suggests power, integrity, bargaining, negotiating, and justice-seeking as being the greater good for the greater number and is more important to men than to women. To women moral and faith development understands intimacy and care to be responsible identity anchors rather than the male's identity which is geared toward individuation, achievement, integrity of selfhood, independence, and autonomy.

Gilligan observed that women consistently concern themselves with the values of care, interdependence, responsiveness and attachment and are less concerned than males with inequality, justice, rights, autonomy, or reciprocity/mutuality.

> . . . Women not only reach mid-life with a psychological history different from men's and face at the time a different social reality having different possibilities for love and for work, but they also make a different sense of experience, based on their knowledge of human relationships. Since the reality connection is experienced by women as given rather than freely contracted, they arrive at an understanding of life that reflects the limits of autonomy and control. As a result, women's development delineates the path not only to a less violent life but also to a maturity realized through independence and taking care.[31]

Studies by Gilligan and others suggest that the differences in psychological and moral development between men and women must be recognized and befriended. It suggests that the complexities faced in dealing with persons dying and grieving can be better approached with an understanding of the variant viewpoints which either ameliorate conditions or militate against resolution of issues faced. With awarenesses of the differences in feeling, thinking, decision making, and taking responsible action, one is better fortified to help individuals and families as they wrestle and struggle to make sense of realities in time of crisis. With such understandings and awarenesses more hope is realized for the preservation of personal identities, autonomy, responsibility, care, compassion, fairness, justice, compromises, values, beliefs, and integrity.

Langdale agrees with Gilligan's insight.

> In structural-developmental theory's fifty-year history the identification of both the justice and care orientations in both males' and females' moral thinking and their representation in theory have only recently become issues of concern. They were raised by Gilligan's (1977) empirical identification of the care orientation found primarily in the thinking of girls and

women and not represented in existing versions of moral development theory. The theoretical insights originating in Gilligan's research, together with Lyons' (1982, 1983) clarification and translation into a methodology for systemically identifying both orientations in moral dilemma data, are integrated in this chapter ("A Re-Vision of Structural Development Theory") with the results from a study (Langdale, 1983) empirically confirming the ethical and epistemological assumptions which define both orientations as structural wholes.[32]

In a somewhat different way, since they are not necessarily concerned with moral and spiritual development, Belenky et al. (1986) provide important contributions to our understanding of the development of self, voice, and mind. *Women's Ways of Knowing*[33] agrees with the contention of Gilligan that developmental theorists in psychology have been men and that women have been largely left out in developmental theory. Women are seen through the eyes of men; women are understood by developmental theorists, if judged by their selection of males only as criteria, to have followed developmentally the psychological and emotional patterns of men. The feminine tends to be ignored. The self in women is largely defined in terms relationally to themselves and other selves while men are more concerned with rules, laws, and principles in making moral judgments, with little emphasis upon relationships and care. While both are concerned about responsibility, men place less emphasis on care and responsibility in approaches to decision-making, negotiating, reasoning, and acting. The understanding of issues in development which women experience and face has been aided and increased by a review of *Women's Ways of Knowing*[34] by Mary Catherine Hasty, a colleague.

She points out that the research of Belenky and colleagues reveals that females have more difficulty in asserting their authority or considering themselves authorities; more difficulty in expressing themselves in public so as to be heard by others; more difficulty in gaining respect of others for the prowess of their minds and ideas; and more difficulty in the utilization of their capabilities and training in the workaday world. Hasty summarizes how women learn to develop in the following.

Perspective of Silence

Women tend to develop epistemologically out of the perspective of *silence*. Women are perceived as "dumb, deaf, and unable to learn readily." Women then are passive, reactive, and dependent upon authority (usually male) which causes women to develop and to adjust to a man's world.

Perspective of Received Knowledge

As women move to a different perspective, *received* knowledge results in beginning to listen to the voices of others and to grow in gaining the confidence that she can hear, understand, and remember knowledge. Even though learning occurs by listening, self-confidence of her own voice has not occurred. Right answers are sought and these are corroborated by the voices of other women as they share and become more confident in learning the commonality of their experiences, thoughts, and concepts. They continue to seek experiences in their search to gain a voice, unaware of how their perspectives may be compromised. Powerlessness and impotence in the face of culture's male authority figures encumbers the process of gaining the inner voice, though this is much sought after and desired.

Perspective of Subjective Knowledge

In the search the woman comes to discover that her own intuitions can be trusted and that right answers can be found within herself, and in her own identity development. The logic, analysis, and even language of males is eschewed. Authority (especially male) is distrusted. The inner authority of the woman and thus her own voice, becomes trusted. Personal autonomy becomes more consolidated and imbedded within the woman and in relationship to other selves.

Perspective of Procedural Knowledge

The movement from subjective knowledge to another perspective involves the growing, developing, more autonomous woman in *pro-*

cedural knowledge. Developmentally and educationally, informal tutors, mentors, and formal educators serve as monitors in the development of an evaluative voice. The critical inner voice becomes louder and the subjectivist voice is lost. More objectivity is experienced but complete separation is resisted. Descriptively, a bifurcation or branching occurs, that of separate knowing and connected knowing. "The predominant theme of separate knowing is knowledge as it implies separation from object and mastery over it. The predominant theme of connected knowing is understanding and involves intimacy, equity, and acceptance."[35] Collaboration and commonality become authoritative. Believing is easier than doubting for connected knowers; doubting, critiquing, and questioning becomes the evaluative mode.

Perspective of Constructed Knowledge

Constructed knowledge recognizes that all knowledge is constructed and carries with it the recognition that the "knower" is an intimate and integral part of what is known since context is important and answers depend upon context. Self-reflection, integration, and articulation characterize this voice and posture. Rigid boundaries are resisted; neat packaging is not productive; intense rationality is not serviceable. It is neither the inner voice nor the outer voice which is normative; it is more that both inner and outer voices are heard and followed.

The authors of *Women's Ways of Knowing* state succinctly the purpose and value of their work:

> We have argued in this book that educators can help women develop their own authentic voices if they emphasize connection over separation, understanding and acceptance over assessment, and collaboration over debate; if they accord respect to and allow time for the knowledge that emerges from first-hand experience; if instead of imposing their own expectations and arbitrary requirements, they encourage students to evolve their own patterns of work based on the problems they are pursuing. These are the lessons we have learned in listening to women's voices.[36]

These authors and others set forth a compelling necessity for us to recognize gender differences in moral and faith development. As these occur in one's own personal psychological, emotional, and spiritual histories in the unfolding of one's own familial history and life narrative, confidence in the woman's self is gained and solidified as authoritative. These distinctive differences are important as pastors minister to individuals and families in dying and death crises, and in taking seriously how the family group itself functions to meet these crises.

ETHNIC DIFFERENCES

In my opinion it is impossible for a white person fully to enter the mind-set, life, and social context of blacks. No white person would presume to understand black soulness, lifestyles, emotions, and heartthrobs. It is important to recognize this and to hope that black caregivers will address the need of facing the black/white differences in the crises of dying and grieving. Perhaps the limited treatment presented here will provide incentive.

In *Roots of Soul*, Pasteur and Toldson (1982) in their Psychology of Black Expressiveness present us with windows for gathering glimpses of "black expressiveness" described as "the readiness or predisposition to express oneself in a manner characterized by vital emotionalism, spontaneity, and rhythm."[37]

> Often these traits act in combination with one or more essential characteristics; naturalistic attitudes, style, creativity with a spoken word, and relaxed physical movement . . . these interact to produce human behavior that when expressed or perceived registers images, sounds, aromas, and feelings of duty to the senses. It is the intensity, duration, frequency and utilitarian features of the behavior, resembling those of traditional African people, which makes it unique.[38]

Pasteur and Toldson propose and offer as psychologists propositions which have been experienced as distinctive differences between whites and blacks. Those acquainted with the arts, sports, politics, contemporary society, socially stratifying processes, economics, and religious practices and beliefs have no difficulty in recognizing distinctive differences. The studies of Pasteur and Toldson clearly indicate that cross-cultural honesty in investigation reveals deeply rooted prejudices based upon misunderstandings, misinformation, pride, paranoia on the part of both blacks and whites, resistance, opportunism, oppressiveness, insecurity, exploitation, and deeply entrenched personal malaise.

Of importance is the distinctiveness by which black persons and white persons, irrespective of gender, manage and cope with crisis and conflictedness. Pasteur and Toldson suggest that:

> A key to the understanding of the method utilized by ordinary black people in managing stress often resides in appreciation of their dependence upon music, movement (dance and athletics), the spoken word (poetry, preaching, "rappin"), styling (the way one expresses his individuality or difference), and profiling (articulating one's difference, usually through movement or showing off) to express the strivings of the soul.[39]

The authors of *Roots of Soul* point out that their terminology referentially is to "ordinary" black people. By "ordinary" black people they mean "common," "average," or sometimes "typical" black people. These terms are used synonymously to describe people who have retained noticeable behavioral characteristics of the African heritage.

Not of insignificant important is the realization that:

> . . . common blacks seem to perceive the environment and respond to it with musical notes (spirituals, jazz, blues, gospel, reggae, samba), movement (dance and athletics), and lines (graphic art and sculpture) more often than whites or acculturated blacks who are more dependent on printed words and numbers in search for consonance with the world.[40]

It becomes clear that these distinctive differences are operative in stress, grief, crisis, and more minor concerns and are dealt with in creative ways which become functional. When understood in the context of dying and grieving, entirely different approaches are both experienced and followed in dealing with whatever crisis does exist.

This is a departure from prosaic, customary, and conventional constructs either experienced or practiced by divergent cultures. Pastors
who seriously intend to give care to the dying and grieving of the
black individual in particular and the black community in general
cannot ignore these differences and are encouraged to develop an
awareness of and become educated concerning the existing differences.

Primordially, blacks are not bound by constrictive categorizations
predominant in Western thought. Defenses are alien; rationalizations
are not important; repression is insignificant; justification is unim-
portant; emotional constraints are absent; and conventionality is
ignored. Expressiveness, creativity, spontaneity, rhythm, and excita-
tion become normative, even ritualistic. Why follow the prescribed?
Or the expected? Or the repressive? Or the constrictive? For the
black to follow white norms is to perjure, to deny, to expunge the
natural and rhythmic. In effect it represents a departure from racial
and ethnic primordial essence and origin. Pasteur and Toldson agree
with Kesteloot in the following:

> Just as whites are indelibly marked in their way of thinking,
> feeling, or expressing themselves by Western European civili-
> zation, whose key values are Reason (for the mind), Technique
> (for work), Christianity (for religion), Nature (for art), and
> Individualism (in the social life), black people are formed by
> their culture, of which we already know the principal traits:
> Solidarity, born of the cohesion of the primitive clan; Rhythm
> and Symbolism in artistic and religious manifestations; Partici-
> pation in the cosmic forces, *"special reasoning processes,"*
> which, although neither prelogical nor alogical, do not neces-
> sarily follow the Western mind or its syllogisms.[41]

Useful to understanding essential differences in perspective and
outlook is "left brain" and "right brain" thinking and action. Left-
hemisphere thinking is contrasted to right-hemisphere thinking. The
left hemisphere looks at tasks in a logical manner, examining,
comparing, and contrasting; right-hemisphere thinking, on the other
hand, is the seat of our creative and artistic capacities, and our
appreciation of form and music. The right hemisphere is an under-
used system of thinking of Western man for it is the left-brain

system which pursues reason and logic. This is a significant distinction to be taken into account when blacks and whites are compared. The white mentality is perceived as that of logic and reasoning, whereas the black mentality is one of spontaneity, creativity, and expressiveness.

Consistent with psychological studies and neurological discoveries:

> The left hemisphere approaches tasks in a logical manner, examining, comparing, and contrasting. Information is taken into it bit by bit, processed in a straight line, logical fashion, and it carries on verbal and mathematical reasoning. . . . It is responsive to material reality.[42]

Left-brain thinking organizes, constructs, patterns, and employs the approach of cause and effect, action and consequence, by a method of chaining together sequential experiences. Decisions leading to action are thought through, deduced or induced dispassionately, and therefore dependent upon facts, reliable information, and learned utilitarian experiences. The author agrees with Pasteur and Toldson who maintain that left-hemisphere thinking predominates in Western man. Such thinking ensures control, security of self, predictable consequences, safety, and adherence to social norms and societal conventions. This may in fact account for Western man's romance with social and political engineering, enamourment with psychotherapeutic approaches, conventional religious order and ritual, and corporate resistance to deviant economic approaches. Such thinking imposes social and religious constraints upon the free expression of emotion and creativity.

Right-hemisphere thinking does not follow such constrictive handling of experience and reality. It does not allow itself to be infatuated or wedded to courses of action devoid of rhythm, emotion, and creativity.

> The right hemisphere perceives images and holistic gestalts. Thinking abstractly, it processes information in a spatial and intuitive way. It uses non-verbal modes of communication involving images of the visual, tactile, kinesthetic, and auditory processes.

It is the right hemisphere thinking which is responsive to spiritual reality. . . . The right hemisphere seems to be the seat of our creative and artistic capacities, and our appreciation of form and music.[43]

Right-hemisphere thinking is experientially sensate and sensual. Characteristically and definitively it is oppositional to left-hemisphere thinking which is more visual than auditory. Different from Western culture with its strong emphasis upon the individual and personal identity, the corporate or collective (the family and group) become considerably more important to un-Westernized black persons.

Group interdependence functions to enhance creativity, to provide a sense of belonging, to reduce anxiety experienced by aloneness, and to give comfort and support in crisis. The collective, representing the interdependency or *oneness* emphasis in the African world, supports the individual, provides for individuals an optimum of personal security, and serves as the most effective antidote to or killer of anxiety. Group interdependency, in contrast to individual independence, functions at a supreme level of creativity. By combining the creativity of the individuals who make up the group, the group extends the capacities of its members, conferring upon them grace, knowledge, and an even greater power of self-expression, which expresses the collective. Invested in the group is a kind of superpower, being stronger than individual members, which helps control weaknesses in individuals standing alone and isolated.[44]

"Blacks are therefore more in tune with the spiritual domain, the rhythm force, and in turn are more vital, emotional, creative, artistic, expressive, and generally less anxious."[45] Black culture in Western life, when it has refused to conform and has allowed itself to revert to its pristine African roots, has provided the world with its rich legacy of jazz, folk music, and folklore. When it has submitted to and conformed to alien influences it has become more customized and less indigenous. To whatever extent black culture has allowed itself to become adoptive of other thought and feeling frames, it has become less possessed of soul and more sophisticated. Judging from the influences of black artists, musicians, poets, dramatists, and athletes, the Western culture white person has come to appreciate rhythm, creativity, and emotion. Doubtless some measure of cultural transmutation has occurred. Perhaps more needs to occur. Rarely can the white person resist the strong and kindred emotions created by jazz and blues; the sounds of the trumpet, saxophone, clarinet, and vocalizations of "When the Saints Go Marchin' In." Soul, rhythm, artistry, and creativity musically and artistically expressed combine to reach deep within the souls of persons who allow soulness to enter life.

> An intensely emotional capacity, expressed together with the human capacities for thinking and movement, was the heritage of every individual of African lineage. Emotionalism is highly valued among African people and rests at the heart of the black folk tradition in other parts of the world. Every black community close to its native heritage was equipped with an emotional-spiritual quality that has made possible the task of 'getting ouvh' or surviving the continued difficulties that life in the West poses.[46]

Slavery, colonialism, industrialization, oppression, and discrimination have caused a transformation, an acclimatization, a modicum of social transmutation and unnatural constraints. Although these have taken a toll in lifestyle and unnatural adjustments, survival would not have been possible had it not been for the profound constitutional equipment of physique, emotion, and soul of which blacks are made. The black capacity for rhythm, emotion, laughter, music, humor, and soulness have ensured survival in the face of arduous labor, menial tasks, social and economic deprivation, personal indignities, injustices, legal inequities, and limited opportunities.

Insights and understandings contributed by Pasteur and Toldson, the author's experiences in the rural and urban Southern United States, rappin' conversations with black friends, and being participant in the dying, grieving, and funeral services with black persons and families collaborate to lead the author to suggest several precepts useful in ministering to black persons who are dying and to their survivors. For facility in understanding and delineating, these are numbered and stated as principles.

First, faith and moral development is inclined in more natural directions and is less sophisticated with black persons than with whites. While inherent in some noticeable and perhaps loosely ordered process (not necessarily in progression) faith and moral development are less rational in blacks and less intellectualized as precepts and beliefs. Nature, not mind, influences faith development in the black culture.

Second, the family system is more closely interwoven in black culture, more interdependent, more impervious to alien cultural influences, less secretive than family system theory suggests is true of white families generally. Survival is a principal motif and is strongly entrenched by previous African history. Despite its acculturated accommodation to white Western customs, survival still remains an indigenous characteristic.

Third, living, dying, death, and grief are accepted as normal. These are embraced as inevitable occurrences and are recognized as a part of the life force itself. While vibrancy and longevity are much desired, dying and death are not as defied, despised, struggled against, or denied. Death in this life gives way to eternal life in the future beyond death.

Fourth, pain and suffering are emotionally experienced to the soul's depth and are strongly expressed as natural processes of life. Death, as with the Apostle Paul, is "reckoned not worthy to be compared with the rewards of the life to come." It is presumed that pain and suffering are a distinctive part of humanness and in fact fit into the scheme of the Creator. These are the common lot of all persons and occur in life as surely as night follows day. These common experiences are woven into the fabric of life and reality, and are readily accepted by black persons.

Fifth, catharsis and emotional release are rituals in themselves and do not need defined structures or binding customs. Permission for vocal or verbal expression is not only given but encouraged by the family unit and larger community. The wake and funeral themselves evidence this value and need.

Sixth, rhythm, creativity, spontaneity, permission, vitality, and soulfulness persist importantly in dying and grieving as in living itself. Life is simply this way. To resist such realities is to resist nature and creation. Uncommonly detrimental results follow the denial of such life forces.

Seventh, music, humor, and laughter contribute to emotional release of raw feelings of pain, suffering, hurt, sadness, and disap-

pointment. These promote comfort and nurturance, becoming vehicles for emotional solace and wholeness of personal and family being.

Eighth, the family finds comfort in the unified belief and faith system through dependence upon God and through its dependence upon the family's unified sense of loyalty and solidarity. Clustering about the family of the dying and grieving is that larger community of faith and support which confers upon and lifts out interactively the common faith which binds these persons together. Intersocially and interfamilially members become able to transcend the sorrow experienced and to believe in the worthwhileness of life beyond the experiences themselves.

Ninth, the funeral service and burial service serve to affirm faith and hope for future life and bind the individual persons and family, the larger family, the church, and the world to each other and to Creator God. Memorial and funeral services help needs to be recognized and grief to be experienced in actuality. In the community of faith those hopes devoid of fear are ratified. In the grief experience, the worth of the departed loved one is captured and celebrated. Failure and futility are buried beneath the strident affirmation of faith that life is wholesome, good, holy, and meaningful.

Tenth, the preparation of the deceased, the death watch, and the wake give opportunity for wholesome grieving and wholesome emotional comfort. Time is understood in terms of timelessness. Clock time and calendar time are not as important as in Westernized culture. This phenomenon has been observed by a number of sociologists (particularly Pasteur and Toldson) and is discernibly noticeable at the time of dying and death for black persons. Blacks take time for grieving. The observance of time limits and restraints is not only nonimportant in black life generally but is considerably nonimportant at the time of one's dying and death.

Chapter 2

Understanding and Usefulness of Family Systems in Ministry to Dying and Grieving Persons

For very good reasons, therapy and counseling are giving serious attention to the family systems of persons who seek help. Significant contributors to this approach with whom I am acquainted have been Murray Bowen, Edwin Friedman, Carl Whittaker, Augustus Napier, and W. Robert Beavers. Their efforts have been a healthy corrective to therapy and counseling which has enabled individuals to make satisfying and productive adjustments to life. If one takes seriously the contributions of family systems theorists, it is virtually impossible to help persons deal effectively with issues and concerns without acknowledging the importance of their families of origin. It is also important to consider the particular family systems which have helped individuals form their values, beliefs, lifestyles, and methods of coping with life and its realities. A grasp of their emphases, understandings, and approaches has much value for ministers concerned with giving help to those who are dying or grieving.

As the minister launches into the important and needed work of ministering to the dying and grieving, the advice of James and Cherry cannot be disregarded, "Before you can help others, you must have resolved the grief episodes in your own life."[1] No minister shall have come to this point in life without having experienced a number of griefs and their backlash.

As I have studied and viewed it, the Newmans' work is informative:

> Psychosocial theory . . . is based upon six organizing concepts: (1) stages of development, (2) developmental tasks, (3) psychosocial crisis, (4) a central process for resolving the crisis of

each stage, (5) a radiating network of significant relationships, and (6) coping—the new behavior people generate to meet the challenges and build the relationships of their lives.[2]

The pastor who wishes to be effective in ministry to dying persons and their survivors is well advised "to go to school" to learn how psychosocial and family systems theories can help. Responsible ministers recognize this as a part of their calling.

The Newmans claim an indebtedness to Erickson who:

> . . . proposed that the stages of development follow the *epigenetic principle*, that is, a biological plan for growth allows each function to emerge in a systematic way until the fully functioning organism has developed.[3]

Further,

> The concept of life stages permits us to consider the various aspects of development at a given period of life and to speculate about their interrelatedness.[4]

A colleague in pastoral care[5] has contributed to my knowledge of physical principles upon which theorists base systems generally and family systems in particular. A major foundation stone is the principle of entropy. Entropy can be described as the tendency of nature and things to go into disorder. Set in terms of biology, tropism is the natural inclination of a plant to gravitate toward light; therefore, the plant moves to the basic source of light, the sun for the planet Earth, to enable photosynthesis to take place. Photosynthesis occurs when the plant utilizes light to manufacture food necessary for its own life and that of other organisms.

Entropism is the inclination to move in the opposite direction for the human organism, for life other than human organisms, and for laws and principles which may be neither human nor biological. Negentropism, the opposite of entropism, is the tendency of things to go into more orderly configurations or homeostasis. While not describing homeostasis in the terminology of negentropism (the tendency to move into orderliness) Menninger, Mayman, and Pruyser understand human personality as a process of moving toward balance. The suggestive image is one in which the person is like a ship in a storm on high seas having within the capacity of righting itself in life's storms. Balance (homeostasis) is sought in the midst of life's realities and crises. The ship is constructed with the capacity to right itself in a storm on the high seas, thus avoiding capsize; similarly the human personality posesses the potential and capacity for "righting" itself in life's storms and seeking balance and wholeness in the face of life's crises and realities.[6]

Low entropy in the family system shows a relatively high degree of orderliness, while high entropy indicates a relatively low degree of orderliness. The goal in family therapy and counseling is to find the points of low entropy. It is important to recognize that individuals possess both flexible and rigid boundaries. Entropic family systems have inflexibility, undifferentiation, ineffectiveness, and failure. The negentropic family system posesses flexibility, autonomy, adaptiveness, and goal achievement potentialities.[7] Therapist, counselor, and pastor become involved in enabling the family system itself to reach the most wholesome level of adaptability to the crisis at hand.

As one ministers to dying persons and to their grief-stricken survivors, it is altogether likely that much of grief work will not be done with an entire family system. It is important nevertheless to recognize the entropic and negentropic valences that do exist and have existed in the family system itself. The goal in family therapy and in ministry to the crises of dying and grieving is to find the points of low entropy, and to lift up and mobilize whatever wholesome residuals of values, beliefs, stability, coping skills, and hopes are present. When this is done with sensitivity and care, both individual family members and the family itself are enabled to deal with and transcend hopelessness and despair.

In the utilization of family systems theory it is important to recognize that:

life is essentially interpersonal;

homeostasis seeks security in the midst of change;

life has radically different causality patterns which are multiple, interactional, and mutual;

limitation of power exists for any one participant, since each person has multiple methods of influencing outcome.[8]

When seeking to enable the family group to move to more wholesome interrelating, effectiveness is achieved through expressivity, self-disclosure, feedback, emotional presence, cognitive connection, and social integration. Ministering to the individual who is isolated from his or her family system may require the minister and person to recognize that the minister or therapist has become the facilitator, participant, and in some sense, surrogate family. Expressivity, self-disclosure, feedback, emotional presence, and cognitive connections are important when the minister is dealing with the whole family, yet he must not lose sight of the individual's needs and personal development.

> Keep in mind that the person is changing on several major levels during each period of life. Tasks involving physical, emotional, intellectual, social, and self growth all contribute to the person's resources for coping with the challenges of life.[9]

It is individuals who grieve—both outside and within their families. Personal emotional development varies despite a family's stimuli.

As understood by Newman and Newman,

> In our view, developmental tasks consist of a set of skills and competencies that contribute to increased mastery over environment. The tasks may reflect gains in physical, social, or emotional skills, or in self-understanding.[10]

To this I would add, spiritual self-understanding. Persons are beings of body, mind, and emotion, but also spirit. The spiritual cannot be ignored.

BRIEF SUMMARY OF FAMILY SYSTEMS THERAPY

As suggested elsewhere, there are several significant contributors to the understanding of the nature of family systems, how these systems operate, their influence upon individuals, and methods for dealing with the dynamics that persist. It is impossible either to include or fully present all family systems theorists. Despite differences in the way systems theories are elaborated and applied, there are common threads of concurrence (Bowen, 1986; Beavers, 1976; Friedman, 1985; Lewis, 1978; Napier and Whittaker, 1980). These are the family systems theorists who have most influenced and informed the author.[11]

When the family experiences crisis it becomes stressed. Families seek to deal with these stressors as they have in previous crises. In some instances, rather wholesome approaches to the existing crisis will be practiced by families who have learned to manage and cope. In other families essentially the same crisis is dealt with in unwholesome ways. The normal response in some families is to seek to identify the crisis and to work toward homeostasis, well-being, resolution of the crisis, and survival. The family finds itself in the state of stasis, its life situation, and the primary characteristic of this family is fear, which causes the family to work toward some solution. The stasis becomes a severe threat to the survival of the family in terms of relationships one to the other as family members. The normal response or reaction is to seek an identified patient (person) or culprit who has caused the family crisis. The family which seeks a level of responsibility (Beavers, 1976; Friedman, 1985; Bowen, 1986) finds itself acting and reacting in a variety of ways to one another. An escalation of emotions commonly occurs, leading the family to place blame upon a particular focal person because they believe this will result in the solution of the concern or resolution of the difficulty and stress.

The presence of emotional volatility causes stress to increase. This results in a polarization of family members within the family unit. Sides are taken and emotional warfare is waged. The central dynamic which follows is triangulation. In extreme instances this emotional triangulation may become so severe that the identified patient or person as focal point may become isolated, ostracized, or verbally and physically abused. Simply expressed, triangulation occurs when two or more family members "gang up" on one or more other persons in the family unit and scapegoat that individual (or individuals). The one person (or persons) is caught in the middle of the interlocking relationship as energy is invested toward reconciling or resolving the problem. The pastor who seeks to help when a person is dying or who is involved in the grief work which follows death sees an enormous flood of emotional dynamics created as families seek to deal with a dying family member or plan funeral arrangements. The pastor sees a previously loving, wholesome, and well-adjusted family become much the opposite. An average minister will remember the strength of convictions which family members express in deciding which hymns will be used, which funeral home, which minister or ministers, burial or cremation, organ donation, postmortem autopsy, and many other concerns. To avoid such conflicts on the part of family members, each person should make these decisions known in a will while still living. Persons die despite the availability of medical care, competent physicians, modernized hospitalization, and good home health care. The crisis of death is ever present and the family is left to deal with critical dilemmas occasioned by it. Some measure of resolution is demanded.

From the smallest family crisis to the most severe, most families have the desire to meet the crisis responsibly. This is relative to the presence or absence of certain family values, beliefs, aspirations, and desires. If responsibility is taken seriously (Beavers, 1976; Friedman, 1985; Bowen, 1986), individual identity becomes blurred and diffused in the interest of preservation of the family unit. Movement toward homeostasis necessitates self-differentiation on the part of the individual. Self-differentiation, Friedman suggests, is the capacity of a family member to define his/her own goals and values apart from other family members.[12] When family members engage in self-differentiation, the diffusion of identity, as understood by Napier and Whittaker (1980), causes each family member to begin to pull together since the family's identity becomes more important than the identity of the individual. In order to avoid becoming disloyal or "rocking the boat," the fear of losing each other causes the family to respond more wholesomely to the crisis. It is stasis or fear which causes the family to pull together and work toward a solution.[13] This choice on the part of the family leads to a reidentifying of the family and the reinstitution of the self into the family system. When purposefully approached and intentionally pursued, the family system meets the crisis, emotional distances are mollified, and homeostasis (balance) is realized and restored. Beavers suggests that goal-directed negotiation is important in achieving reconciliation.

Each family has many problems to solve. In rating the capacity of a given family to solve problems, two aspects are important.

The first has to do with the efficiency of the family in arriving at decisions; the second has to do with the degree to which the family encourages negotiation among all its members. Dysfunctional families are quite inefficient at solving problems. Other families with lesser dysfunction deal with problems efficiently, but without true negotiation, and the family response to a problem usually reflects the work of an overtly powerful family member. Optimal families solve problems efficiently, relying on family negotiation to arrive at solutions. Solutions represent the best the whole family has to bring to problems.[14]

In the face of this, family secrets (Friedman, 1985) must be addressed or subterfuge occurs and direct, open, goal-negotiation is sabotaged. Secrets militate against honest communication and preclude optimal resolution. In bringing family secrets into the open and addressing these, individual autonomy necessarily must be protected and honored. Necessary ingredients for the optimal achievement of desired results include acceptance of the value of each person's identity and opinions, the unconditional love of each for the other, the spirit of nonjudgmentalism, and refusal to engage in blame-placing. While the task in helping families to face the death of another and working with the bereft family is exceedingly difficult, it is not impossible. Such ministry is in no sense always easy to accomplish. Despite the difficulties, the effort is worthwhile.

USEFUL CONCEPTS OF FAMILY THERAPY IN MINISTRY TO THE DYING AND GRIEVING

In ministry to the dying person and to the family through the dying process and the grief following death, employment of several principal understandings of family systems is useful. *First, it is important to survey the family field of the nuclear family as well as the extended family.*[15] How does the family relate? What are the family's patterns of relating? How has this family met crisis or conflict in the past? How does it seek to meet these crises or conflicts in the exigency of the present moment? How does the family operate? These become questions of significance for the pastor.

Assessment of the family system is necessary. Sensitivity, reality, reflection, intervention, involvement/detachment, and cognitive empathy are important qualities for the pastor's approach. Both mental astuteness and compassionate caring are important ingredients of the interrelationships with the troubled family and its individual members. What does the pastor know about the allegiances which exist one for the other? What are this family's values and beliefs, and what coping skills have been observed and can be noted about the family? These are important concerns. In this respect, the pastor who has had long-term relationships with the family is fortunate.

One of the inhibiting difficulties pastors experience is the tendency to be directive, to give advice, and to project into the family system the pastor's own beliefs and manner of coping with crises. Although hard to resist, the pastor's task is to enable the family to arrive at its own approaches to resolve concerns.

A second important principle is the determination and character of triangles and alliances in the family system. The triangle refers to the "three-person" system, that is, the smallest stable relationship existing. "The triangle has definite relationship patterns that predictably repeat in periods of distress and calm."[16] The triangle normally results in a twosome that is comfortable with a third and less comfortable outsider. Alliances are thereby formed and emotional loyalties develop. To evaluate the strength and nature of these is important. Appropriate intervention is necessary. Strong and effective triangles and alliances militate against a wholesome solution and likely sabotage the achievement of homeostasis.

Buying into unwholesome triangles and alliances on the part of the pastor is detrimental to achieving homeostasis. Dying and grieving families seek other allies. Unless the pastor is careful and astute, it becomes easy for the pastor to be triangled into the interrelationships of family members. This further complicates interfamilial relationships. Constructive, wholesome adjustment to loss by the family is more likely achieved when detachment and objectification by the pastor is valued and practiced.

Knowledge of the total family configuration of the dying person in the family and the overall level of life adaptation are important for anyone who attempts to help a family before, during, or after a death.[17]

Clearly the work of enablement by the pastor involves one in remaining outside the web of family entanglements. Facilitation of the process is the important function and cannot be realized when the pastor becomes triangled into the family web.

A third important principle is the observation of patterns of participation and nonparticipation of family members. To what extent can individuals in the family be brought to take part in the solution of the crisis? How close or how aloof are family members, how impervious is the family system to change and adaptation, how strong/fragile is the family, and who are the dominant or stackpole persons in the family? It is of value to look for the polarities, the individual identities, the family identity as a whole, and the functional autonomy of individual persons in the family. This may lead also to determining dependency, independency, and interdependency valances and dynamics operating within the family. Intervention and prodding of nonparticipating yet significant family figures may become necessary.

The pastor is faced with the task of determining his or her participation and nonparticipation in the death crisis with which the family is grappling. For the pastor who has become intimately involved with the family over a considerable period of time, resistance to counterproductive involvement can sometimes be interpreted by the family as one's being callous or unconcerned. Growing out of the minister's role in society, especially in more geographically provincial contexts, it is not an easy task to "participate" and "not participate" all at the same time. The pastor who is not sufficiently secure may tend to dominate or referee. Where a long-standing relationship exists between pastor and family, the esteem and respect in which the pastor is held by the family can sometimes foster unwarranted dependency or faulty choices. Unwittingly the pastor may be tempted to become a part of the extended family or an extension of the community canons and codes.

Fourth, an important principle in family systems management is the differentiation of self and the ego mass. Bowen (1986) suggests that each family makes up an ego mass, which refers to the collective mass of several ego units—parent, parent to parent, parent to child, child to parent—all of whom contribute to the experiences which form this awareness and how these experiences interrelate. How have individuals determined themselves as selves in the context of family relationships? Some knowledge of the individuals' identity, their sense of autonomy, their awareness of their own personhood, the health or unhealth of self-esteem in individuals and the family unit, as well as the sense of personal importance family members have within the system itself is useful. Awareness of the relationship to the system by each individual is critical.

Sometimes new stresses are brought on by the terminal illness or death of a person. Earlier marital conflicts resurface, poor interfamilial relationships between children and parents emerge, and the dysfunction of one member (identified patient) may reappear, causing emotional and religious problems. Crises as extreme as dying and death can become the tinderbox which causes otherwise well-kept secrets within the family to burst into flame. Beavers (1976) holds that "mythologies" exist in families. He cites as examples of family myths: "Father is only interested in his business; mother is a saint without any hostility; one child is spiteful and mean, while another is always kind and cheerful."[18] These need to be recognized as distortions that are shared by the family and which have become "secrets" that have been kept from the larger, extended family or community or pastor. Most families function in ways that cause their corporate ego to fabricate a family personna as a hedge of protection against those outside the family. Much energy in families is geared toward making the family look good no matter how unhealthy familial relationships might be. Doubtless the outside community's perception of the family is always at some variance with what the family seeks to project to the outside world. During the crisis times of dying and death the family is likely to put much energy into preserving its family myth or secret. Does the minister then ally with the family to protect this image or does the minister bring into the open this undisclosed mythology? Neither. The wise pastor will be aware of the need for the family to protect itself and will respect the family's identity. He will be mindful also of the detrimental effects that such myth perpetuation has upon later grief work.

A fifth useful guideline in grief work is the recognition of grief dynamics. Reference is made to my chapter on understanding grief. Most ministers have experienced what Bowen, in his helpful chapter "Family Reaction to Death," calls the "emotional shockwave."[19] The "emotional shockwave" is a network of underground "after-shocks" of serious life events that can occur anywhere in the extended family system in the months or years following serious emotional events in a family.

> It occurs most often after the death or the threatened death of a significant family member, but it can occur following losses of other types. It is not directly related to the usual grief or mourning reactions of people close to the one who died. It operates on an underground network of emotional dependence of family members on each other. The emotional dependence is denied, the serious life events appear to be unrelated, the family attempts to camouflage any connectedness between the events, and there is a vigorous emotional denial reaction, when anyone attempts to relate the events to each other.[20]

Of significance, says Bowen, are the position of the deceased in the family, the emotional attachments existing, and alliances and/or secrets that exist. He contends that not all deaths have the same importance to family members.[21] Where the deceased family member was positioned in the family is important: father, mother, child or children, as well as the power and prominence of that family member in the system. It is important to recognize where the dying or deceased person fits in the family system. How dependent or interdependent are or were the family members in reference to the dying or deceased person? Was this a newborn or was this person the breadwinner, the resourceful and stable mother, or the wayward, rebellious teenager?

Since the pastor by calling, by function, and by role occupies a place of prominence second to none, and since the pastor is often regarded as the custodian of morals, values, and beliefs, when persons are dying or grieving, families quite often are dependent upon the pastor to help them make sense of the experience. The insecure minister is likely to take advantage of this position of power and influence. The temptation is to move in forthrightly and to attempt to bring order out of chaos. In family systems terminology this is to help the family move from disequilibrium to equilibrium, stasis to homeostasis, and fear to survival. To be entrusted with such a position of power can easily become ego-satisfying and self-serving, but is a temptation to be resisted. "Life-cycle events present the minister, rabbi, priest with unusual opportunities for working with families and individuals within the family unit."[22]

Friedman (1985) lifts up values and functions of these spiritual helpers such as using the long-term relationships with family, treating the crisis as opportunity to affect the entire relationship system, serving as "coach" to the family and individuals, using the triangles that form around the clergyperson therapeutically, optimizing the possibility of long-term comfort by not anxiously rushing to supply a short-term balm, among others.[23]

The pastor will recognize how important it is in grief work to determine the openness/closedness of the family system; to keep himself abreast of understandings of grief itself and the family system through observation and assessment; to seek to intervene appropriately and therefore help the family to objectify reality; to accept the limitations of the family system itself as well as one's own self; to be persistent over a long period of time as equilibrium and homeostasis are sought; to be mindful of the ego mass and self-differentiations involved; and to both understand and enable emotional, mental, and spiritual skills to be implemented and utilized. The pastor who is threatened by the task, who feels inept in understanding the family system, or is in jeopardy of losing the pastoral relationship with the whole family or its individual members may feel inclined to refer these persons to a family therapist. This may well be the better course of action provided the pastor remains in spiritual and emotional support of individual persons and the family itself.

Chapter 3

The Pastor's Ministry
to the Dying

It is always a shattering emotional experience for a person to learn that he is dying. We have no precise way of knowing the wide range of emotions that are stirred up within each individual person, since each person is different from every other person. The realization that death is near is frightening. When family members learn that one of their own faces death, it both catalyzes certain emotions and paralyzes other emotions. The nurse, physician, or clergyperson who seeks to help a dying person should expect a variety of emotions to be displayed by the individual.

To learn that a patient is terminally ill is a terrifying experience for those responsible for his physical, emotional, mental, and spiritual care. It is a sacred time and an opportunity for bringing comfort and strength. Although the minister may feel inadequate in this most difficult of pastoral ministries, the shirking of this task inevitably leads to feelings of guilt. It becomes necessary to develop emotional strengths to learn to deal with one's own feelings, and to apply whatever emotional and spiritual insights are at his disposal for utilization and practice at this tragic time.

THE NECESSITY FOR SELF-UNDERSTANDING

An awareness and utilization of the minister's own feelings is basic to the effectiveness in working with dying patients. Feelings of anger, grief, frustration, ambiguity, fear, and depressiveness can block him in his ministry to dying patients. Unless he is careful, he too will engage in denial mechanisms within himself and and find it hard to face the reality of the death of one committed to his care. We must face our human finitude in the dying of those to whom we seek to minister. It helps to remember that this is a pertinent reminder of our own humanity and frailty. It is important to know that in our grieving for ourselves we could fail to consider the feelings of patient and family. The pastor may deny his own humanity so much that this becomes a cover for his false image of sufficiency. Insufficiency is perceived as weakness, lack of faith in God, or underdevelopment of one's religious life. Since feelings are powerful motivations to action, self-honesty is important. First of all, it helps to admit these feelings and have the ability to identify precisely what these feelings are. Once identified, one is then able to objectify and use the strength of these feelings to help someone else. It is helpful in aiding such identification of feelings if the pastor has someone with whom he can air these feelings—preferably someone other than a family member or spouse. It is valuable for the minister to have a "confessor," a friend who takes him seriously, but at the same time helps him to be objective. It is helpful to discuss impasses and concerns in a group of fellow ministers, provided they take themselves and each other seriously. Identification of feelings as well as objectification of these feelings becomes important. Through self-knowledge and group reflection, the pastor is better able to cope with the feelings which other persons are experiencing at the time of dying or death.

Mills' words are worthy of consideration by the minister.

> When one confronts American society's tendency to deny death and to isolate the dying and the bereaved, it becomes apparent that the pastor's presence is needed still. Strangely enough, many contemporary pastors are defensive about their work in this area. They feel that the medical profession cares for the dying and the funeral director cares for the bereaved.[1]

There are several reasons to justify the presence of a minister at the time of terminal illness. What are some of these?

By virtue of his theological education and his own personal faith in God, it is appropriate for the minister to be present. The minister's faith experience places him in the role of a source of support for the dying patient. Many times he is the primary support system. This is true not only of his religious support but also of his ability to be of emotional support. It is imperative then to have come to terms with a meaningful, viable faith by which he can personally authenticate spiritual sustenance. So important is a realistic faith that the minister must seriously grapple with religious and spiritual realities in order to avoid giving churchy, pious answers to the vital questions of life and death. In the face of the crises of dying and death, some ministers unwittingly revert to primitive, kindergarten-type ideas of God and of the life to come. It is morally reprehensible to engage in intellectual sophistry and urbane cliches when someone is at death's door.

He is justified by his calling, his personhood, and his role as representative of God to be present with the dying. In the everyday experiences of life, persons image the minister as a clarifier of reality, a diviner of heavenly mysteries, an expert in spiritual matters, a confessor, a pastor and friend, and professional religionist. Since this is so in the day-to-day activities of living, how much more so at a time when someone is coming to the conclusion of his life.

Mills emphasizes the importance of the pastor's function by saying,

> By understanding the needs of the patient and the bereaved, and by the grasp of his own heritage and Christian faith, the pastor may serve to help break down the barriers that anxiety about death continues to raise.[2]

Inherent in his calling is his own self-awareness and the church's awareness that he is especially spiritually fitted, is a careful student of the ways of God, and is a steward of the "mysteries of God." It is important that his calling be underscored by his own personal commitment to the development of his authentic personhood and his faith system. When such is true, he functions out of his own uniqueness as a person, and therefore what he does and who he is convinces those to whom he is ministering that he is "in touch with God." While no one can go all the way through the valley of death with another person, the minister can at least walk part way. The need for community by the dying person calls for the assurance that he does not go into this experience alone.

The support system which the minister becomes to the patient and family is another justification for his presence with the dying. The spiritual maturity which he has developed and the emotional stability which he has cultivated help to objectify and give perspective to death. It is expected that he has developed spiritually and emotionally to the point at which he can be depended upon by the patient for support in the uncertainties with which he is assaulted. Unless the minister is willing to develop this kind of maturity and ability, he forfeits the right to be called upon at this critical time in a person's life.

UNDERSTANDING AND USING AVAILABLE SUPPORT SYSTEMS

Theologically, the Judeo-Christian perspectives on man's nature emphasize the importance of viewing persons holistically, i.e., as body, as mind, as spirit and emotion. The practical implications of this are obvious. The minister will take the patient seriously with respect to his mental, physical, emotional, and spiritual life and nature. Since the well-being of the whole person is involved in his dying, the presence of all health care specialists is important. By nature of the crisis, physicians, nurses, allied health specialists, psychiatrists, social workers, and ministers have their functional roles.

Additionally, the Judeo-Christian emphasis upon the corporate nature of personality demands that all significant persons involved in one's dying be both a part of his dying and play strategically important roles in his dying. Important to an understanding of roles is the serious consideration of all aspects of the dying one's personhood. Personality attributes and needs of the patient and family members to be identified include the following:

- the health status of the family members
- available family income
- primary moral religious and ethical values of the family
- family standards for good and bad
- significant shifts in roles of family members

- identifiable patterns of communication
- social status of the family in its own eyes
- the community's viewpoint of the family's social status
- the strength and value of the community, family, and religious supports.[3]

The family must be dealt with as a whole. This of course includes the patient himself. Such family involvement enables therapeutic purposes to be achieved. Total family involvement helps each family member to take part in the care of the terminally ill and enables the survivors to give the ministrations unique to his own personhood. It helps to distribute the feelings of responsibility for the care of the dying patient and enables family members to accept and live with the success or failure of the patient's life. Thus, no one family member needs to feel guilty for having failed other family members or the patient. Family involvement enables survivors and patient to have firsthand contact with each other in ways that are mutually meaningful to them and provides consistency in dealing with grief for the survivors. The minister can help them face the realities of the death of the patient.

The perceptive, candid, moving book, *Living with a Dying Man*, pseudonymously written by Jocelyn Evans (1971), tells the very personal story of her husband Aaron's death. After only six years of marriage, Jocelyn Evans learned that her husband, then thirty-three, was dying of cancer. Their first faint inclination that something was wrong occurred when the couple left England to vacation in France, ironically, the scene of their honeymoon and of so much happiness. There followed the interminable round of medical examinations, hospitalizations, operations, the final diagnosis and the long weeks of nursing, caring, and fighting for hope—despite the implacable odds.[4] She writes passionately about her own personal pain, her frustrations with the impersonalized practices of her husband's employer, and the dehumanizing protocol of the medical profession, and society's superficial attempts to comfort. She encountered resistance from her husband's physician, Dr. Warfield-Scrogge, who discouraged her from taking her husband home.

In the days after Aaron was able to leave the hospital and to go home, she heroically devoted herself to giving medication, to easing his pain, and to caring for his needs. It gave her immense satisfaction to be able to spend these last days with her husband and was doubtless, meaningful for him too.

> Aaron spent a large part of his last days in those days of life at home in relative comfort. Just before Christmas he said, "On Christmas Day you must all come into my room, all of you." Perhaps he was going to make Christmas after all. I thought it was a pity that Dr. Warfield-Scrogge was unaware of what was going on.[5]

For medicine, ministry, community, society, or family to deny a spouse or family the right to personal preferences is an unjustified and unforgivable travesty.

EMOTIONAL DYNAMICS AND RESPONSES OF DYING PATIENTS

In working with dying persons there are concerns, dynamics, and responses necessary for one to consider.

The dying patient tends to deny the reality of approaching death.

The nature of death itself as well as our own natures make it hard to face. We simply do not want to die. The whole idea of dying is resisted. Death is repugnant and it is reasonable to expect to surface. The will to live is far stronger than the will to die. Denial is the common emotional response to the primal drive to live.

The dying patient has concern for those who are left behind.

This is common in fathers and mothers for their children, as well as children for their parents. The dying person attempts to gain meaningfulness by extending himself through other persons of his flesh and blood. This is normal.

Unrealistic dealing with the factual reality of death robs both the patient and those around him of significant and meaningful experiences which they could otherwise have with each other. Denial and avoidance preclude the social intimacy of verbal intercourse of spirit with spirit. Open communication of words and feelings go far toward alleviating the fears and terrors of death. Candid communication also lessens the psychic and emotional disturbances which death occasions. Also this manner of communication helps to condition and sustain all those who are suffering through the crisis and experiencing it.

The dying patient may wish to talk to someone about his past life.

Anyone in the medical or ministerial profession may be a part of this conversation from time to time. In the process of dying, persons often engage in flashbacks, idealization, or fantasies. "The dying patient's request for meaning and completion may also be hindered by a sense of failure. The knowledge that unfulfilled tasks are left often leads a young or middle-aged person into bitterness."[6] Elderly people especially tend to go back to earlier days to talk about some of the meaningful experiences of their lives. To listen to some of the thoughts and ideas expressed may seem trite and inconsequential. However, these moments of reliving the past are exceedingly important to the one who is talking about his own life.

Feifel (1959) feels that

> . . . one of the serious mistakes we commit in treating terminally ill patients is the erection of a psychological barrier between the living and the dying. Some think and say that it is cruel and traumatic to talk to dying patients about death. Actually, my findings indicate that patients want very much to talk about their feelings and thoughts about death but feel that we, the living, close off the avenues for their accomplishing this.[7]

Hendin (1973) would agree that, "Our embarrassment at the individual face of death forces the seriously ill and dying patient to live alone on the brink of an abyss with no one to understand him."[8] Hearing the dying person out helps keep him connected with the worthwhileness of life and family.

The dying patient often exhibits intense preoccupation
with religious and spiritual concerns.

This is commonly true of middle-aged and older persons though not altogether. God-talk involving the religious vocabulary of "sin," "failure," "repentance," "salvation," "heaven," "hell," "the Lord," "the Church," are common religious referentials. Other religious concepts may come into the conversation. It is proper that these become a part of the exercise of talking out the concerns of life as a person is dying, since these issues are of ultimate importance to him. Each crisis one faces in life is an ontological crisis. As a pastoral theologian I contend that each crisis is a theological crisis. By its nature, crisis forces one to wrestle with ultimate value and ultimate meaning.

Tillich (1959) has observed that man "always lives in a conscious or unconscious anxiety of having to die." "Non-being" is present in every moment of his "being." Suffering, accidents, disease, loss of relations to nature and man, loneliness, insecurity, and weakness are always with him.

> Ideally, a person's preparation for this last great "rite of passage" should begin long before the experience of dying. However, the process of death is almost imperceptible as retro-gressive changes in the organism lead to old age.[9]

The dying patient frequently expresses his fear of death. Not only does he fear death itself but the process of dying is a major concern. All persons desire to die with dignity. Mitchell (1972) suggests, "We hope that in our dying we will prove true to ourselves, true to the way we have sought to live."[10] In a real sense, death is an embarrassing experience. How one will bow out of life assumes great importance. Questions such as, "What will happen to me?" "What will happen to my remains?" "In what way will I be remembered?" repeatedly go through the mind of the dying.

Faber (1971) says the following:

> We hope for a humanly worthy death, i.e., that we shall not pass away like animals, unaware of what is happening. To be more specific, we hope to die in full awareness, having taken

leave of those around us, having our affairs sorted out. We hope for a death which will measure up to our ideals by which we have sought to live. We hope for a death which will match our beliefs.[11]

The dying patient sometimes verbalizes the fear of being totally alone in death.

Much of our lives are lived as social beings and fear of being alone runs deep at a person's time of facing death. While there are those who want to die alone, by far the greater number of persons are afraid that they will be by themselves as they die.

Perhaps the most important lesson the pastor can learn about the dying is of their fear of isolation and of the tendency of American society to segregate them. Dying persons are not as much afraid of death as they are of the process of dying. They fear progressive isolation, and they fear being forced to go at it alone.[12]

This fear can be alleviated if another is beside him in his dying moments. This gives the dying an emotional guarantee and assurance that his remains will be safe for a little while, and that in some sense his remains will be treated with sacredness. Hendin makes a worthwhile point:

Indeed, while modern medicine has done a great deal to help overcome physical pain, it has accomplished precious little in the way of easing the final burden of loneliness. The dying must face the possibilities of emotional pain, grief, and indignity—and they must face them alone.[13]

Whether or not modern medicine is the sole culprit is questionable, since medicine's practitioners are joined to a culture which handles dying poorly. His indictment applies to others as well.

The dying patient experiences certain regrets about his life.

Quite often he takes a look back and second-guesses himself over decisions at certain critical junctures in his life. He will find himself thinking about how he could have improved his life and how he might have been of more service to his close friends and family and to the larger circle of mankind. In quite an opposite way he is likely to talk about some of the successes and some of the meaningful experiences and achievements of life. The likelihood is that he will say far more about the regrets of his life than the successes he has enjoyed. Patients are heard to say something like, "I wish I had it to do all over again. My life would be different."

The concerns of a dying patient need to be taken with utmost seriousness. In his chapter, "Death,"[14] Mitchell talks about an experience with an eighteen-year-old girl and her frustrations about not having experienced what many others had and how she wanted to savor all of life there is before she died, as well as thoughts about dying at home rather than in the hospital. She also gives evidence of wanting to talk about life after death in her future conversations with the chaplain. Of importance is the quality of relationship which the hospital chaplain gained with this patient and the freedom with which she was able to talk about such significant things as wanting to have intercourse before she died, of wanting to square things up with some of her friends, of talking about the ultimate issues of life and death, and about her preference for not dying in an unreal and artificial way. He talks about the meaningfulness of their conversations as she was released from the hospital to go home, the stages through which she passed until a final acceptance and the freedom with which she talked to him about still being a virgin, and about her coming to the place of acceptance by talking about what was meaningful to her. She was enabled to take a measure of control by virtue of decisions she had made for herself during her illness. She was able to accept the fact that she would die, never having had the sublime experience of intercourse. Through a no-nonsense, realistic, viable, and caring relationship that he had communicated to her and to other patients, he was able to enter into the struggles through which they were passing. His ability to communicate in a caring manner enabled him to become involved in the meaningfulness of the experiences which surfaced during their dying. The conversations he records are of value to anyone wishing to develop a caring ministry to dying persons.[15] There are occasions when the minister can help persons look at their feelings of regret and let them verbalize their concerns by asking the simple question, "Suppose you did have it to do over again; what is it that you would have changed?" Frequently persons talk abut specific matters, but often there is vagueness about their regrets. From the perspective of the listener they may seem quite trivial, but are real to the dying patient. He ought to be given the opportunity to verbalize these concerns. Undoubtedly this is an extremely inexpensive luxury for someone who is breathing the last breaths of life. When the conversation does turn to critical and serious matters, it is reassuring and comforting to the dying patient to be able to find someone who will take seriously the regrets he is experiencing about his past foibles, indiscretions, sins, failures, and inadequacies, as well as his successes, triumphs, moments of glory, and achievements. "Death is a multifaceted symbol. The specific import depends on the nature and fortunes of the individual's developmental and his cultural context."[16]

> In conclusion, a man's birth is an uncontrolled event in his life, but the manner of his departure from life bears a definite relation to his philosophy of life and death. We are mistaken to consider death as a purely biologic event.

> The attitudes concerning it, and its meaning to the individual, can serve as an important organizing principle in determining how he conducts himself in life.[17]

Dying is never easy. In many cultures death represents futility and failure. It is seldom greeted warmly and generally signifies pain, disappointment, and incompleteness regardless of a person's age or accomplishments. In our Western culture it can be made easier than in the past for dying persons and their families when honest confrontation with death occurs.

"The great majority of people do not leave life in a way they would choose. In previous centuries, men believed in the concept of *ars moriendi*, the art of dying. . . . We live today in the era not of the art of dying, but of the art of saving life, and the dilemmas in that art are multitudinous.[18] Nuland contends, and few would disagree:

> The dignity that we seek in dying must be found in the dignity with which we have lived our lives. *Ars moriendi is ars*

vivendi: The art of dying is the art of living. . . . Who has lived in dignity, dies in dignity.[19]

Undeniable and unequivocal truth.

In our own country the pioneer efforts and successes of Dr. Elisabeth Kübler-Ross have resulted in fresh and new awarenesses of how death can be better managed. She has been a significant teacher for many who have taken seriously her learnings from dying persons. All who are concerned for dying persons and their families are in her debt.

Another important development in caring for the dying is the hospice movement. Its genius lies primarily in its comprehensiveness and compassion. As far back as medieval times, hospices were in operation as a way station, a concerned community, providing a place for refreshment and replenishment, as well as renewal and care, for sojourners. Doubtless the sick and delicate were left there interminably, some being left even to die. For better than four hundred years the sensitive consciences of caring people caused them to initiate communities whose mission it was to provide physical relief, emotional support, and spiritual nurture. As Sandol Stoddard (1978) in her eminently informative and consummately thorough study of the origins, the developments, the uniqueness, and the importance of hospice points out:

> Of all the threads that illuminate the substance and the fabric of this time, one leads directly to St. Christopher's Hospice in London, 1967. Following its path we can move through four centuries of time, touching people who knew and touched one another and looked into one another's eyes, over the span of some thirteen generations.[20]

Although several European precursors manifested and utilized certain concepts and practices in giving care, it is Dr. Cicely Saunders to whom the credit is given for originating the modern hospice movement in 1967 at St. Christopher's Hospice in London. Taking the compassionate former models, she developed a program of comprehensive care for terminal patients and their families. In preference to prolonged treatment and management in hospitals, often involving considerable expense of energy, emotions, and finances, programs of hospice care came to offer alternative health care focusing upon the easing of physical pain, provision of emotional support to patient and family, and spiritual sustenance. Hospice philosophy has never sought to become a substitute for needed medical care, but has valued and practiced the humane manner of helping terminal patients and their families when continued conventional medical care and treatment no longer was possible.

From the first clearly specified elaboration of hospice care at St. Christopher's still others came into being in England and on the continent. The hospice concept came to be appreciated and applauded in America as a sensible, viable, and needed approach to the terminal. Programs of considerable substance and vitality came into existence in New Haven, Connecticut, St. Luke's in New York, Marin County, California, and Royal Victoria Hospital in Montreal. Its astonishing development can be traced in Dr. Stoddard's work, *The Hospice Movement,* to which reference has already been made. In less than two decades from its formalized beginning with Dr. Saunders, hundreds of hospice programs are providing care. The movement has grown from a few local programs into a national group called National Hospice Organization. The small brochure of NHO defines it:

> Hospice is a specialized health care program emphasizing the management of pain and other symptoms associated with terminal illness while providing care for the family as well as the patient. Medical care for the patient is coordinated by physicians who supervise a team of professionals, including doctors, nurses, psychiatrists, or psychologists. Other patient and family needs are attended to by social workers, clergy, and trained volunteers—both before and after death.[21]

The concept of hospice as stated by the mission of Hospice of North Carolina, Inc. is a philosophy and method of care which stresses the management of pain, psychological and social support for the person and family, care in the home and institution, care by teams of professionals and trained volunteers, bereavement follow-up, initiation of palliative intervention, and the meeting of spiritual needs of the person and family. Member and affiliate groups of National Hospice Organization, as for example, Hospice of Winston-Salem/Forsyth

County, Inc., subscribe to and maintain a program of care, including the following:

> A hospice care program considers the patient and the family together as a unit of care; hospice provides continuity of care; hospice services are physician directed; the goal of hospice care is the prevention of distress from chronic signs and symptoms; hospice care is provided by an interdisciplinary team; hospice care is available on a 24-hour-a-day, 7-day-a-week on-call basis; hospice care for the family continues into the bereavement period; hospice utilizes volunteers as an integral part of the interdisciplinary team; hospice programs have built-in means of providing support to the care-giving staff. Admission to the hospice program of care is dependent on patient and family needs and their expressed request for care. There is no discrimination on basis of race, ethnic origin, religion, or ability to pay.[22]

In hospice care new and innovative ways are being developed nationwide. In keeping with Hospice's promise that care will be provided at home, or in the most homelike environment possible, Hospice of Winston-Salem/Forsyth County, Inc. has embarked upon building Hospice Home, a free-standing facility to accommodate twenty patients and services for patients and families. The two primary hospitals have pledged financial support, along with businesses and industries. Hospice is committed to "Adding Life to Every Day." Hospice care, wherever and in whatever way its ministries are developed and elaborated, responds to the critical need of patients and families consistent with the sentiments of a former professional colleague, the Reverend Ronald Mudd, a Hospice patient:

> There are times when medical science, despite all its skills and buildings and equipment, simply cannot add more days to people's lives. It is then that Hospice can add more life to their days.

It cannot be too strongly recommended that the pastor become knowledgeable about hospice programs in his community and to support these in appropriate ways.

EMOTIONAL PROGRESSION
IN THE DYING PATIENT

Phases of emotional progression in the dying patient are clearly identifiable. In her pioneer work *On Death and Dying*, Elisabeth Kübler-Ross became a teacher to so many. Her categories of emotional and mental responses and expected attitudes provide structural awarenesses of what the dying patient is experiencing. Anyone who deals with a dying patient or the bereaved family is well advised to consider carefully her studies with the dying. She deals with denial, anger and depression, hope, bargaining, and acceptance in her descriptive categories. Especially pertinent to pastors, if responsible care for dying patients is given, are the concepts of hope, bargaining, and acceptance.[23]

First, the stage of hope. Unless the minister is cautious he is likely to be unrealistically forward in the matter of giving the assurance of hope to the dying patient. There are times when one's theological understanding of God's power and love can lead him into giving unrealistic assurances. While ministers generally believe that God has immense powers for healing, an honest evaluation of the way God normally functions would indicate that there are many times when it does not appear to be God's purpose to heal everyone. It is important for the minister that he not destroy a patient's hope. It is also important that he not be guilty of encouraging false hope for the patient or the family of a dying patient. Often the pastor's zeal to be helpful leads him to overly reassure. One needs to be careful not to foster a hope that has little or no basis in reality. To do so can be very injurious to the faith system of the patient or the patient's family.

The minister often is vulnerable when the patient talks wistfully about miracle drugs, advances of medical science, and new breakthroughs in the treatment of his own particular illness. Medical knowledge and healing skills have pushed the frontiers to a point of hope that taxes credulity. Common sense should keep one from going too far in unrealistic expectations. In his declining days the terminal patient may read newspaper articles or his friends may tell him of some recent new discoveries that have been made in illnesses similar to his. The patient may put stock in the possibility that this will become the cure for him also. While it is unwise to take away this element of hope for the patient, one should steer away from giving false hope.

Second, the stage of bargaining. Usually the bargaining is with God along such lines as, "If you will let me live until my children are grown, I promise you that I will be more faithful to my church" (or religious fellowship). Bargaining may take the form of promises to God, for the dying patient's desperate plight brings out both his need to live and his need to live meaningfully. Nonreligious persons sometimes bargain in theological terms. In desperate circumstances one wants to reaffirm life, to perpetuate one's own existence, and to add meaningfully to the ongoing of the race. Even though God-language itself may not be present, there is frequently strong determination to continue to live and to contribute to life. While in nonreligious terminology, one regrets certain past deeds and is quite anxious to mobilize his resources toward making a contribution to those around him and toward maintaining a meaningful existence for himself, frequently this is not possible.

Third, the stage of acceptance. Some of the frustrations that attend the dying patient center upon his inability to be in control of his living or his dying. Many persons are religiously content and satisfied. They feel secure about their relationship with God and do not question this satisfying relationship to him. However, even those who have settled matters religiously may still be very much confused and troubled emotionally. The emotional acceptance of one's death is far more difficult than is his spiritual acceptance of peace and serenity. The emotional acceptance should become a major focus in one's ministry to the dying. Frankl has suggested, as I understand him, that meaningful existence is what makes life worth living. In both *Man's Search for Meaning* and *The Doctor of the Soul*, Frankl stresses the importance of one's finding meaningfulness in the living of our lives to make life worth living.[24] It is normal for the dying patient to struggle for meaningful existence in his life as he comes to an acceptance that his life is coming to an end. Elderly persons often engage in long resumes of their past lives. They may talk about many meaningful experiences; they may talk about happy experiences and sad experiences; they may talk about their failures and their successes. But this does not belong solely to the elderly. Whenever any person comes to the awareness that his life is almost over he recounts the many varied experiences of his life. This is one of his ways of assessing the value and meaning of his life to himself and to others. This sort of reminiscence is healthy and satisfying. Emotionally, this means a change from denial to acceptance. Although not in control of his life, at least the dying patient recognizes that there were times when he was in fuller control of his activities, his thoughts, his feelings, his lifestyle, and his destiny. To some, such recounting may seem morbid. But there is considerable emotional value for the dying patient to be able to talk about some of the wishes he had for himself before his life is over. Conceivably there are certain things that he wishes to have done after his death. All of us live out our lives with certain preferences. We have certain preferences about such things as memorial services for ourselves, method and manner of burial, whether or not to be interred in the family burying ground or cremated. There may be other wishes dear to the one dying, and it is good when these can be talked about with members of the family, with a minister, or close friends. While such ideas as this may sound strongly suggestive of giving up or of looking forward to death, the failure to engage in some significant conversation with those who are meaningful to us could also reflect how deeply entrenched is our denial of death. To be clearer, if the dying patient takes the lead and gives out certain clues which indicate that he would like to talk abut his preferences, his frustrations, his fears, or whatever else is of concern to him, there should be someone available who will engage in meaningful conversation with him. Should the dying person wish to deny his death down to the last moment, he ought to be given this privilege. Should he wish to talk about death, those who are with him in the last weeks and days of his terminal illness should be aware of his need so as not to fail him at that critical time. Hendin (1973) cites the instance of a terminal patient dialoguing with her physician who, upon hearing her doctor honestly admit that she was dying, said: "Well, I've finally broken the silence barrier. Someone has finally told me the truth."[25] There have been patients who have said, "I so much appreciate your talking with me about my dying." "You are the only person who has taken me seriously enough to listen to me." "I have tried to talk with others and they simply gave me the run-around and would not let me say some of the things that I have said to you." The studies of Hackett and Weisman (cited in Hendin), Harvard psychiatrists, conclude that dying patients should be told the truth. They found that all the patients they studied had suspicions of their coming death, though they had not been told it. "All patients were relieved to have their suspicions confirmed."[26] Dying patients deserve the right and privilege to be taken seriously.

It is far better for all if the dying can conclude their life on this earth in meaningful dialogue with significant persons than to be "cut off from the land of the living" before physical death claims their bodies.

HELPFUL PRINCIPLES FOR THE PASTOR

Whenever possible it is advisable to make contact with the patient before the extreme crisis is reached so that more meaningful help may be given. Oates (1964) notes that the pastor whose relationship with a patient has been only fair before the crisis cannot make up for this deficit by becoming compulsively concerned about his salvation all of a sudden.[27] This involves the consistent visitation of parishioners and members by the minister in order to build the kinds of viable relationships that can be useful at times of dying and death.

The minister must possess a strong religious confidence in God's loving care and his consistent concern for his creation. Of immense value is cultivation within one's self of a faith system which has significance for the minister himself. This faith system cannot be built upon superficial platitudes about the goodness of God and the goodness of life.

The pastor is well advised to make short, frequent visits with the patient. The patient often gets lonely even with his family close by him continually. So often family members protect each other at crisis times and the process of dying is no exception. One should avoid the pitfall of making long visits unless there is good evidence to indicate otherwise.

Showing signs of grief by the family is realistic and responsible. While it is dishonest to play games with the dying patient, the minister can show his concern for one who has told him about his imminent death and should not go into panic as death is talked about. While this is not an easy task, there is value in letting the dying person know how meaningful his life has been to others and to the pastor himself.

The patient should be encouraged to take the lead in discussing religious matters. While this is difficult in that the patient's family may often expect the minister to "get him saved," one should avoid trying to coerce the person into a faith relationship simply because it will make the family feel better. It is unfair and pointless to attempt to force a patient into a relationship in a short time when he has had his lifetime to make a religious decision. Skill is involved in encouraging the patient to talk about his faith. When the pastor is patient, it is interesting to see how soon a patient who knows his illness is terminal will move toward religious discussion.

It is always good to be alert to the patient's desires and signs suggesting his wish to confess secret sins. At such a time it is often necessary to ask all other persons to leave the room so that he has the privacy to express whatever may be weighing heavily upon his heart. In *The Dynamics of Confession,* published by John Knox Press, I have dealt with the matter of guilt and confession. I suggest the minister concern himself with the material in this book.[28] The pastor, whether he desires it or not, is frequently cast into the role of confessor when a person nears death.

Common sense indicates that one should not whisper inside or outside the patient's room. This gives the patient the idea that others know more about his condition than he does. It is unfair to the patient and is a breach of honesty. When it is necessary to talk with the family members it is better to converse with them at times and places other than the vicinity of the patient's room. A nod or a gesture is enough to let the family know that you would like to talk with them.

Exercise care in cases when the patient does not know that he is dying. He may ask, "Am I dying?" and when this does surface, it is good to refer him to the doctor by simply asking him if he has talked with his doctor about this. Many times the way the patient phrases the question is a good clue as to how much he knows about his condition. When the patient says, "Isn't it true that I am dying?" generally he is aware already that his condition is growing worse and death is close. If he should ask, "You don't think I am dying, do you?" one may safely conclude that he is not ready yet to deal with the closeness of the time of death.

Be completely honest in your own province. The minister is not medically trained and cannot know precisely when a person is actually dead. It is not within his province to tell a patient that he is dying unless he does this as a request of the physician himself. Deception is unfair, unjust, and dishonest, and we can help the patient more by telling him there are others with whom he can talk about these concerns. Avoid unrealistic reassurance. When the patient has been told how ill he is, it is dishonest to seek to reassure him against the inevitable.

There are several problems which a minister faces in dealing with dying. These may be phrased as questions.

First, what does the patient know about his condition? The answer to this question involves the doctor, the nurse, the staff, and the minister. It is important that the minister check with the professional medical staff to determine both the patient's knowledge about his death as well as the prognosis concerning the time that he can expect to live. Another vastly important consideration is whether or not the patient is continuing to deny his death or if he has come to accept the fact.

Physicians are not at all unanimous in their opinion as to whether or not a patient should be told about his coming death. It is a highly individualized matter. Physicians generally decide upon this after weighing the factors with each patient. The important consideration is that the pastor ascertain what the patient knows about his prognosis from the physician himself.

Second, whose responsibility is it to tell the patient? It is the doctor's responsibility. The next question for the minister is: "How much has the doctor told the patient?" When the question about imminent death is asked the minister, it is always better to ask, "What has the doctor told you?" By no means should the minister tell the patient he is going to die, unless it is either in the presence of the doctor or at the explicit request of the doctor.

Third, how does the patient feel about his death? Once the patient has made this an agenda, following upon the suggestions heretofore that the patient should take the lead, it is altogether appropriate for the minister or chaplain to ask the patient, "How do you feel about this?" "What does dying mean to you?" "How can I help you face this crisis?" The minister must strive to be with the patient in his concerns and to learn to hear the great variety of answers. Many patients will be afraid, many will deny this, many will have moved to a tacit acceptance, and many will be confused about it. It is important to help the patient explore his feelings about this. As listener, clarifier, and empathizer, the pastor's role is of real significance.

Particularly when one is ashamed of feelings which for him indicate weakness or unworthy thought, it is well for him to attempt to share these with understanding, accepting friends, relatives, or professional counselors. There is no real merit in canceling such feelings. The clergyman, especially one who has added skills and personal counseling to his religious training, may well be the one to whom the person with a deeper problem may turn.[29]

Fourth, what is the patient's spiritual relationship to God and what are his relationships to other persons? Medical personnel and staff have their special function during these trying days but there is no one who stands in the unique position with the dying patient or the bereaved family in quite the same way as the minister. It is to him that they address questions about the ultimacy of life; it is with him that they talk about the meaningfulness of their lives; and it is with him that they voice their hopes and fears about what lies beyond death for them. So it is important that the minister is secure in his value system, his faith system, and his theological beliefs. It is never wise to attempt to superimpose one's own faith system upon another; the patient's own faith system is of vital concern. Many questions will be put to him concerning life after death, one's relationship to God, and one's relationship to himself and those he is leaving behind. Since the minister by role is God's representative, the dying patient finds comfort and strength in verbalizing concerns, anxieties, aspirations, regrets, and fears. The minister is likely the only person with whom the dying person seriously grapples with ultimate concerns.

AIDS: THE DISEASE

Pastoral care of the dying cannot be complete without addressing AIDS, its complexities, its devastation, and its need for creativity in approach. Physicians and scientists who have studied AIDS (Acquired Immunodeficiency Syndrome) have discovered that "[v]ictims of the disease manifest a puzzling array of previously obscured diseases: rare cancers, a lethal form of pneumonia, and other uncommon and life-threatening infections."[30] It has become clear that these diseases arise as complications (sometimes symptoms) and diagnosable diseases of a single underlying disease: the immune system itself breaks down and involves physicians in treating opportunistic diseases which arise out of somewhat multiple diseases commonly experienced by persons who are not AIDS victims. The immune system is so exquisitely and intricately designed that under ordinary circumstances protozoal infections can be controlled by the system itself. When this happens, the growth is controlled, little or no threat to life is posed, and the human organism remains healthy and intact following the safeguards intrinsic in the immune system itself. According to Mizel and Jaret (1985), pneumocystis or carinii resides in most persons and is not so controllable with those patients who have AIDS, since pneumocystis is responsible for a lethal form of pneumonia.[31]

Toxoplasma gondii also is commonly found in the human organism, and studies have shown that more than half of the adults in the United States are infected, with that number rising in certain subpopulations. In adults who are healthy the immune system successfully controls the growth of toxoplasma. In AIDS patients, debilitated infants, and individuals undergoing immunosuppressive drug therapy for malignancy or organ transplants, this protozoa, toxoplasma, can cause toxoplasmosis. The danger of such a condition is an infection of life-threatening nature occurring in the central nervous system. If this parasite invades the placenta and infects a fetus, it can lead to mental retardation or blindness.[32]

Sufficient information is becoming common knowledge for the person who is interested in making an educated investigation. Newspaper articles and a report by the (then) Surgeon General, C. Everett Koop, MD, have been published as a public health service document on Acquired Immune Deficiency Syndrome (October 22, 1986). This author does not intend to deal thoroughly or scientifically with the research that is daily occurring in attempts both to know more about AIDS and to seek to control this dreadful disease. Our entire population must necessarily involve itself in seeking and implementing this knowledge. (The reader is encouraged to become acquainted with the sources mentioned here, as well as many other available resources of information and research. Much is being learned about AIDS and this body of knowledge increases day by day through workshops, seminars, symposia, books, pamphlets, and thorough approaches taken by hospice groups, the American Red Cross, state health agencies and local mental health centers, hospitals, city and county governments, and the United States government. The CDCP (Centers for Disease Control and Prevention) in Atlanta provides continuing help with its wealth of information. It is presently known that AIDS is a fatal disease; that medical care is costly; that no known cure has been found; and that drugs for dealing with AIDS are being developed for treatment, some with promise and optimism.

It is known also that all persons infected are capable of spreading the virus sexually (heterosexually or homosexually) and by sharing needles or syringes or other implements for intravenous drug use. An astronomically high percentage of those infected will develop full-blown AIDS and the medical community predicts that enormous health care costs will severely burden the economic structure. Scientists caution that those with the AIDS virus will develop an illness that fits accepted definition of AIDS within five years. Protective measures must be taken by both homosexuals and heterosexuals, as well as hemophiliacs and intravenous drug users. Despite moral convictions to the contrary, the use of condoms in intercourse and restraint from intravenous drug use presently offer the surest hope of avoiding the disease.

AIDS is a condition which damages the immune system, the body's defense against disease. The damage resulting opens the body to attack by infections and cancers that are not a threat to healthy people. AIDS is caused by the Human Immunodeficiency Virus or HIV. While not everyone who is infected with HIV develops AIDS, others develop what is known as ARC or AIDS-Related Complex. AIDS is caused by a virus that is transmitted only by direct and intimate contact with infected body fluids, primarily blood, semen, and vaginal secretions. Casual contact does not cause a person to contract AIDS, contrary to what some misinformed individuals believe.

The HIV is transmitted by unsafe sexual practices, the sharing of needles, and through blood transfusions of infected blood or blood products (extremely rare since blood donations are carefully screened for signs of the HIV infection). AIDS virus is not highly contagious and cannot be spread through air, food, or by casual contact at home, work, or school. Although a devastating virus once a person becomes infected and is diagnosed, comparatively it is a weak virus.

Langone's work, *AIDS: The Facts*,[33] provides up-to-date useful information about the nature of the AIDS virus, its transmission, symptomatology of AIDS and ARC, present treatment modalities and methods, and precautions for the general population and health care providers. He explores scientific investigations now in progress for arresting the disease, possible cures, and prevention. Langone contributes helpful data for the person who wishes to look in-depth at the disease and the scope of the problems encountered in facing this serious health menace.

PASTORAL CARE TO AIDS PATIENTS AND FAMILIES

In ministry to the AIDS patient and family those understandings in working with terminal patients and their families and of grief are useful. There are additional considerations to those which commonly are expected to occur in addressing terminal illness and death. With AIDS patients it is necessary to go beyond concepts which have been recognized as classic approaches to dying and death. Concerns exist that are specifically unique in the care of persons with AIDS. Along with the present knowledge of this dreaded disease is the awareness that there is no survival rate; presently there are no known survivors to live beyond a few years, and no known cure. Hopelessness and certainty of death pervade.

Clustered around this dread disease are a vast number of fears. These fears are experienced not only by patient and family but community and all of society. There is the fear of contagion despite the number of precautions taken by the medical community, patient and family, and awareness that the virus itself, as viruses go, is quite weak, unable to live outside the human body and the blood system, quite unlikely to be transmitted other than through body fluids, and not known to be transmitted through casual contact. Still there is a paralyzing fear of contagion. When contracted it follows the course of unmitigated devastation to the human body.

So rampant are fears that some hospitals and extended care facilities have been reluctant to accept AIDS patients. Other fears include the loss of civil rights regarding housing, employment, exclusion of children with AIDS from public schools, and the termination of health care benefits. To date the most susceptible persons for the contracting of AIDS are hemophiliacs, intravenous drug users who swap infected needles, homosexual males (female AIDS victims number considerably less), bisexual persons, and promiscuous heterosexuals. The most tragic and pathetic AIDS victims in our culture are those infants and children whose disease has been transmitted to them by their parents who have been involved in destructive lifestyles and practices. Elisabeth Kübler-Ross's book, *AIDS: The Ultimate Challenge*, is an important resource.[34]

It is more acceptable to families, society, and terminal patients themselves, for a person to become ill with cardiological disease, cancer, sickle cell anemia, and other terminal illnesses than it is for society to accept a person who innocently, accidentally, or as a result of habits of lifestyle becomes ill with AIDS. Persons who become terminally ill with diseases other than AIDS do not experience shame to any degree as severely as AIDS victims. Fear of exposure of a private or hidden lifestyle pervades the steps, the feelings, the thoughts, and the entire ethos of the AIDS patient within our society. Although AIDS may be innocently contracted, the implications of drug use, homosexuality, or other unacceptable lifestyles become suspected. When a family member becomes ill with AIDS, oftentimes "coming out," coincides with the news of the catastrophic illness. This leads to internalized conflictedness and secrecy.

Associated with the sense of shame is guilt. For the homosexual, feelings of guilt arise because of having to expose or having exposed a lover, spouse, or friends. Since society generally regards the AIDS patient as having practiced lifestyles unacceptable to society, the AIDS victim experiences guilt for having transgressed the person's own morals and religious values as well as those of the family and society.

The AIDS victim is caught up with the experience of isolation and abandonment. This occurs in family relationships and is compounded by the family's inability to accept both the disease, the terminality of life for the victim, and questions which arise about the lifestyle practiced by the victim. There are health care professionals who shun and intentionally avoid taking care of AIDS patients. Former friends and both business and social associates avoid the AIDS victim. The nature of the disease necessitates isolation for the protection of others and to safeguard against transmission of deadly and devastating viral infections to other patients. This contributes to the isolation felt by the AIDS patient. As disease progresses, the victim experiences a "wasting away" syndrome which severely alters a formerly virile physique.

It becomes necessary for the AIDS victim to alter sexual expression, although there is continued need for such expression and intimacy. This is especially true in the earlier phases of the disease. Fears surface concerning the potential infectious nature of sexual activity. Feeling isolated and abandoned, the AIDS victim becomes concerned about a lover, a partner, or one's own spouse.

Human spiritual and religious needs being what they are, the AIDS victim often finds his own theology inept and unusable. Previously learned theology and spiritual practices become for many limited resources in addressing the disease or the lifestyle of the person. The family also experiences considerable religious/spiritual confusion and hopelessness. The practiced theology of persons with AIDS either stops or becomes less useful as a resource when the religious community or church rejects the AIDS victim out of its own constricted theology about how to relate to this person. It is necessary for the victim to reframe theology, beliefs, and values to achieve religious support and regain faith when death is imminent. The reframing is also necessary for family and friends, for church, for community, and for pastor. The pastor must assume responsibility for assisting the patient and others in the reframing process.

One of my colleagues, Cynthia T. Morse, OEF, a pastoral caregiver, who in 1993 had worked with AIDS/HIV persons for seven years, observed correctly that "suffering is a given, an integral and unavoidable part of the human condition."[35]

As I have cared for them pastorally I have been privileged to enter into that suffering with them and there to be an incarnation/embodiment of God's love and compassion just as each of them has been an embodiment of the divine for me.[36]

Suffering, to me, is at once and the same time a spiritual, emotional, physical, and mental malaise and condition in which the whole being is traumatized significantly. One is forced to deal with realities that bring new and unwelcome experiences that cause pain, raise questions, baffle us, and give us few answers. Suffering reaches into us and hurts. Medical confidentiality, medical treatment, recording of the death certificate with the cause of death, and individual privacy become concerns for the AIDS patient. Fear of exposure is a significant concern. Who will know? How much will they know? And how will I be remembered? These become central questions to the AIDS patient. Will previously undisclosed and well-kept secrets about oneself become public knowledge? The pastor can be of assistance to the patient in covenanting with the medical professional caregiver to safeguard the privacy of the victim.

The present "state of the art" with AIDS patients recognizes the high costs of medical care for the AIDS patient. Data about financial costs changes almost weekly. Drugs which do not cure are unusually expensive. The financial and emotional costs of AIDS are beyond comprehension when one considers job loss in later stages of the disease, status in the family and community, the seriously eroded self-esteem of the victim, and the loss of benefits in employment.

Staff support groups and counseling support for nurses, physicians, and others to deal with stress and burnout, as well as the loss of the patient by death, become significant considerations. Revision of schedules for health caregivers, days off to enable health professionals to cope with their own stresses, protective measures and precautions for surgeons, nurses, caregivers, as well as additional equipment for the care of the AIDS patient add up to considerable expense. Additional training for medical personnel and staff is involved. Wider, more comprehensive treatment plans increase costs to the hospital and health care system. Individuals and society are confronted by what Elisabeth Kübler-Ross quite accurately calls *AIDS: The Ultimate Challenge.*

The pastor has no choice but to become involved. He is a part of the lives of patient, family, community, church, and society. The role and function of the pastor by nature is to become involved in the lives of those persons being served. The pastor is confronted with these issues: disability and fear of death; management of anger, shame, guilt, and loss of control; dependency, stigmatization, estrangement, isolation, and abandonment; completing of life and "unfinished business;" relationships to self, to family, to God; self-esteem and worth as a valued person; reframing of beliefs and theology; and personal confusion and inner conflictedness.

How does the minister provide the needed spiritual support? How does he relate to the moral dilemmas presented by AIDS? Perhaps no issue or concern in this generation presents more challenge to the pastor with so few sure answers to ministering to those persons. The author ventures these suggestions and considerations as at least a place of beginning.

1. It is necessary for the pastor to come to terms with his own attitude and approach theologically and spiritually. One has no choice.

Morse holds a wholesome stance for the minister and with which I agree:

> Informing this task of articulating the theology that informs and drives my work are my own experience of the human/human and human/divine interaction within the pastoral relationship, my theological Christianity and my affinity with the Latin American and feminist theologies of liberation.[37]

If one fulfills his calling, it is mandated that the pastor grapple seriously with his limited knowledge, his confusion, and the contradictory emotional and spiritual ambiguities within. Dependency upon one's own sense of security, personal and professional identity, and depth of relationship to God and to his religious community provide stable relationships and spiritual sustenance. A fellowship and support group of professional peers helps to uphold and to give reality reflection.

2. The development of courage is necessary in the face of unique difficulties encountered with the disease, the patient, the family, the community, and the religious fellowship or the church which one serves. Not everyone will understand. One who follows the example

of Jesus the Christ follows the model of him who defied religious institution, society, and custom. Jesus "went about doing good." The outcasts, the lepers, the adulteress, the underprivileged, the prisoner, the exploited, the poor, the needy, the guilt-ridden, the pauper, the estranged, and all those whose lives were burdened in any way became the focus of his ministry.

3. The pastor will recognize his responsibility to patients, to families, to institutions, to community, and to church. In all strata of corporate life, education about the disease, fears, its presence, and its threats to human existence are emphasized. The pastor cannot avoid the responsibility of facilitating knowledge and educating persons who find themselves ignorant, fearful, and confused.

4. Sensitivity to the needs of all persons concerned and involved in the treatment of AIDS is important. While sensitivity may be a deeply ingrained characteristic in the minister's personality, no terminal disease more severely tests the minister.

5. Out of his own sense of security, that minister is called upon to determine his posture to others in patient/family relationships, community, health care facility, church, and society. It will require soul searching. One is faced with value clarification, confusion, and ambiguity. The author embraces and practices Morse's philosophy, "My methodology is based on relationship."[38] I am persuaded nothing we say or do is more important than relationship.

6. It is essential to trust one's self as a mature and confident minister whose help and support is from God, his personal faith, his church, or his religious community. Risk taking, adventuresomeness, and the possibility of being misunderstood or ostracized may cost the minister. Can the minister become as fearless and courageous in addressing this disease and its victims as in confronting issues of race, nuclear disarmament, corporate exploitation, political disenfranchisement, or any other social or religious issue?

7. It is important to recognize one's role as minister to whom patient, family, and caregivers can turn for help in those theological and spiritual dilemmas posed by AIDS. The pastor is the one religious figure people depend upon in spiritual crises. No one else occupies this position in culture and society.

8. The minister who deals honestly with his own personhood, calling, and position will become more comfortable in his availability to patient, family, caregivers, and community for support, encouragement, and the expression of feelings, attitudes, and fears. It is incumbent upon the minister to function as educator and as facilitator of communication.

9. Historically and culturally ministers have been recognized and respected as spiritual advisors in matters of morals. They have been depended upon to serve as monitors to the religious community and to assume leading roles in determining conscience. Presented with moral decisions involving AIDS, the pastor's advocacy role cannot be avoided. Once again the minister's prophetic and pastoral voice needs to be heard and guidance needs to be given. Informed educational approaches are mandated. The dangers of unsafe sexual practices and drug use cannot be ignored.

Langone affords practical suggestions to persons who seek to be meaningful to AIDS victims.[39] A summarization of a brochure prepared by the Chelsea Psychotherapy Associates of Manhattan, meant primarily for the gay community, follows. The suggestions given are relevant to religious laity and ministry.

- Do not avoid him. Your involvement instills hope. Be the friend and the loved one you have always been. But call before you visit since he may not feel up to a visitor at that moment. Call back.
- Touch him. A simple squeeze of the hand, or a hug, can let him know you still care.
- Cry with him, laugh with him. These intimate experiences can enrich you both.
- Do not be reluctant to ask about his illness. And do not confuse his acceptance of it with defeat. Acceptance might give him a sense of his own power. Also, do not feel that you always have to talk. It is okay to sit together silently, reading, listening to music, watching television, holding hands.
- Help him feel good about his looks if possible. Tell him he looks good, but only if it is realistic to do so. If his appearance has changed, do not ignore it. Be gentle, but do not lie.

- Include him in decision making, no matter how simple or silly the decisions may seem to you. He has lost control of so many aspects of his life.
- Tell him what you would like to do for him, and if he agrees, keep any promises you make.
- Be prepared for him to get angry with you for no apparent reason, even though you have been there and done everything you could. Do not take it personally, and be flattered that he is close enough to you to risk sharing his anger and frustration.
- Do not lecture or be angry if he seems to be handling his illness in a way that you think is inappropriate. He may not be where you expect or need him to be.
- Take him for a walk after knowing his limitations; get him to his doctor; bring a favorite dish; call and ask for a shopping list; offer to help answer correspondence. Offer to do household chores, but do not do for him what he can do for himself. Ask before doing anything.
- If you are religious, ask if you could pray for or with him.
- Send a card that says simply, "I care."
- Talk about the future, tomorrow, next week, next year. Hope is vital to him.

Chapter 4

The Pastor's Ministry to the Grieving

Death is an ignominous intrusion into our lives. Death is unwelcome and forces us to make radical adjustments. The pastor needs to understand its meaning. Death and grief cannot be ignored. Death constantly dogs our steps. We learn constantly of death by newspaper, telecast, word of mouth, and personal experience. We acknowledge the fact of death intellectually and it is experienced emotionally when it comes home to us. So long as death comes in the form of a faraway plane crash, an earthquake on another continent, the assassination of a president or social leader, or an unknown citizen in the city of our residency, death can be managed at arms length without extraordinary difficulty. It is more comfortable when we can keep it that way. But one day it happens: Death comes to one who is as dear to us as life itself. Suddenly we are involved personally in a crisis of grief, sorrow, pain, and loss. We are face to face with the villain, death, which traumatizes one's very being. There is no retreat, for its finality is thrust upon us and cannot be changed.

Everyone experiences grief in one form or another—the loss of a loved person, a most cherished possession, estrangement, separation or divorce, and many other significant losses. One must come to terms with that death in whatever form it presents itself. Once it has come home to us, grief is then a part of our own humanness.

> Grief is essentially a deprivation experience. We lose—or have taken from us—something that we cherish and do not want to give up . . . Death is the most acute form of deprivation experience can take. Not only do we lose what we love and cherish, we also feel that some important part of our own being has been taken away in the act.[1]

It has been said, "Bereavement is another crisis in the life of every person who takes the risk of loving someone other than himself."

The following practical definition helps to explain its nature. Grief is an emotional state occasioned by separation from a loved person or a loved object. Richard McKay, a former associate, has put it this way: "Grief is interrupted love." It brings a heaviness or heavy feeling following a broken relationship with a person, place, or thing. Grief is characterized by loneliness, helplessness, frustration, regret, and finality. It both leads to and needs appropriate expression. As my neighbor, Tom, has put it, "Grief will not kill you; you only wish it would."

In describing the nature of grief, Jackson (1963) says that mourning usually takes three different forms. Sorrow is the first of these. We mourn for the person who no longer is a part of our world, and at the same moment we mourn for ourselves, for our personal loss. We feel loneliness, emptiness, a painful sadness at having to face life without the person we have known so long and loved so deeply. Distinctive sets of feelings cluster around our fears and anxieties. We are faced with sudden change. We are not sure what lies ahead. Many feelings have to do with very practical matters. We wonder what we are going to do next—where we will live, how we will pay our bills, how we will find for ourselves some security in a world that has suddenly changed so drastically. . . . Sometimes we are required to make decisions by ourselves—decisions that were always shared before. This in itself may make us feel insecure and uncertain.[2]

While death is the most excruciating and traumatic loss that one suffers (life cannot be replaced, while things can be replaced), we also need to recognize that many experiences in life are grief-producing. When a businessman goes to his place of business to find it in ruins by fire or explosion, he experiences grief. He is cut off from the symbolic representation of his life work and livelihood. When a church or synagogue is burned, grief follows. As this work was being prepared, a number of church fires occurred throughout the nation, particularly in the south; the nation was shocked by the explosion of an intercontinental airliner in which long-term employees lost colleagues who were crew members, and a small Pennsylvania town lost promising youth, as well as family members and friends; a hurricane in eastern coastal towns brought the loss of homes and businesses. When a family is awakened in the middle of the night by smoke and fumes, runs from the home and watches it go up in flames, deep loss is felt; the child loses a puppy or kitten, a favorite toy, a stolen bicycle, or other object of love, the pains of loss and grief are experienced. The loss of a part of our body by accident or surgery as evidenced by a woman who has experienced mastectomy, the male who loses a testicle, or the young person who loses an arm or leg by surgery, causes that person to go through the long process of loss, hurt, and grief. The loss of a partner through divorce or separation causes grief. For whatever reasons a couple becomes estranged, both husband and wife experience grief in the death of the relationship. When parents separate, children go through loss and grief. Moving from one place to another in job transfer or by causes necessitating such a change occasions grief on the part of all the family members. Ministers who move from one church to another, even with the challenges of a new situation and new people, find themselves grieving for those they left behind. When one loses a job grief is experienced. Broken engagements evoke grief. Grief may occur when persons move from a house they loved and years later return to find the house has either burned down or has been replaced by another house or building. The failure of a young person to achieve his potential brings grief. A daughter who becomes an unwed mother brings grief to her parents over the disappointment experienced. An unwed mother often experiences grief when her child is put up for adoption or when the child's father does not fulfill his promise to marry her. The young man who invests his savings in a new automobile experiences grief when some weeks later he has an accident which demolishes the car. The experience of retirement commonly causes grief. Parents feel grief when a son or daughter joins the armed services, leaves for college, or gets married. These experiences wrench the soul and tear at the spirit and emotions of a person; the pain is very real. For a male the loss of potency causes grief. Young persons, sensitive to their own failures and achievements and their need for peer approval, would be expected to know grief when they fail to make the football team or to become a cheerleader or for other reasons, are forced to drop out of school for a session or semester or permanently. These and many other experiences in life put the focus upon the kinds of heart-rending occurrences that can occasion grief. So it is not simply the loss of the person or the loss of part of oneself that occasions grief, but separation from or loss of anything dear to us that sparks deep feelings of regret, remorse, and hurt. Grief, then is a pain of mind, of soul, of spirit, or body, which comes from some deep trouble or loss and in which one's relationship to a person or thing is broken.

Grief is a normal experience when losses occur, and is a universally painful experience. Jesus himself grieved, as we are made aware by the gospels. "Jesus wept" (John 11:35). The context in which this verse occurs makes it clear that Jesus wept because Lazarus had died. He wept also over the city of Jerusalem out of his deep sorrow and disappointment.

We tend to abnormalize grief and to play it down, but in fact it is quite normal. If we have loved deeply, we grieve deeply. Only the persons blighted by incapacity to love deeply are spared the deep pain of grief. Even so, they pay the price of denying their own humanness.

Clemons (1994), in *Saying Goodbye to Your Grief*, provides a model of understanding grief, and provides a model similar to my work and that of Westberg (1962). In his chapter, "The Anatomy of Grief," he speaks of experiences which bring grief: The death of someone to whom you are bonded, divorce, loss of a job, moving away from your place, someone leaving home, loss of aim or identity, a birth defect, surgery, illness, and loss of a dream or opportunity.[3] He identifies the following as stages in the process of grief: shock, numbness, alternating between fantasy and reality, flooding of emotions and grief, selective memory and stabbing pain, and acceptance of loss/reaffirmation of life.[4] His emphases are extremely informative to the pastor.

Having suggested a definition of grief, and its normalcy, what feelings and feeling states are present? It must be remembered that not everyone experiences all of the emotions and reactions alike, or to the same degree, or all of those mentioned. When we encounter a person in grief and seek to minister to those in grief, the following can generally be observed and looked for in normal grief reactions.

Confusion

Confusion is experienced. The ambiguities and the contradictions that exist within us in our physical and emotional makeup contribute to the state of confusion that is almost always present. We do not know what to make of the event which occasions loss. We are looking within and without for some way out of our confusion. Since our emotions are generally rather intense, we find a conflicting number of emotions being experienced. Sometimes these are contradictory to each other, sometimes they are correlative to each other.

Acute Distress

The grieving person experiences acute distress accompanied often by tightness of throat, spasmodic breathing, rapid pulse, or distinctive contractions of abdominal muscles, among others. Clear and specific physical symptoms are discernible. No serious dealing with grief and bereavement could be attempted without recourse to Erich Lindeman's pioneer work (1944) in this area. His article entitled "Symptomatology and Management of Acute Grief"[5] is helpful in understanding what the grieving person experiences. He suggests the presence of definite psychological and somatic symptomatology. The grief experience may become exaggerated, delayed, distorted, or successfully resolved. Such psychic phenomena would include sighing, lack of strength, physical exhaustion, digestive problems, a sense of unreality and detachment from others, preoccupation with the deceased's image, guilt, intense distress, and evidences of inner tensions and hostilities.

In the small book, *Good Grief*, Westberg (1962) distinguishes several stages through which a person passes, and his stages provide much help in identifying the grief sufferer's emotions and need for their release. These stages include a state of shock; a time for the expression of intense feelings through crying, talking, verbal abuse; feelings of depression and loneliness; the onset of certain physical symptoms of distress, reactions of panic, hyperactivity; the feeling of guilt over the loss, hostility and resentment; and the inability to carry on normal activities.[6] Irion (1954) points out the reactions of tearfulness, bewilderment and loneliness, fear, ambivalence, hostility, guilt, and idealization. Taking these factors into account makes it necessary for a pastor to be involved in evaluating the needs of the bereaved individual, as well as the feelings which may lead him to certain interpretations of the needs of the parishioner that may be different from his own feelings.[7]

Emotional Expression

A pronounced need for emotional expression is present. Frequently grieving persons cry. The need for crying is a primitive emotional expression which occurs spontaneously. Although the need exists, oftentimes the shock is so great that some persons are unable to cry. They are stunned, and thus crying comes later rather than at the moment when the loss occurs. Along with the need for crying are other emotional responses as well, for example, swearing, shouting, hysteria, or even laughing. The author distinctly remembers the emotional outburst of a wife whose husband had just died. When the physician told her this, she broke into laughter and said, "That's the funniest thing I've ever heard." It was funny in the sense of its strangeness and unexpectedness. It is helpful to remember that we can anticipate varieties of verbal and emotional outbursts.

Lack of Muscular Power

A grieving person lacks muscular power. Grieving persons experience dysfunction of normal body movements. Those who work in a hospital setting, or ministers who have conducted funerals can remember well how some persons are motionless when death is announced. The person is not able to ambulate under his own power. Pastors remember grieving family members at memorial or funeral services who are so incapacitated by grief that they need physical assistance into the place of the service as well as help in carrying out simple tasks that in normal living present no problem.

Lack of Reality

The grieving person experiences a sense of unreality about life. The news of death or loss is so incredible and intolerable that one may say over and over again, "I cannot believe it." "It simply is not true." "I will not believe that he is dead." I recall the grieving father and mother of a six-year-old daughter who had been prematurely and tragically killed by a falling tree. In sitting and talking with this friend and his wife in the kitchen of their home, the words kept coming back from this distraught father, "It is so unreal! It is so unreal!"

Feelings of Distance

The grief-stricken experience feelings of distance from others. They do not believe that anyone else can come into their grief world and experience the depth of their feelings. Though family members and neighbors may be physically near, the grieving individual feels that these persons are miles away emotionally. The grieving person doubts that anyone can feel what he or she is feeling.

> Much of the warmth goes out of your relationship to other people. You realize that friends and acquaintances are trying to be helpful, but their expressions of sympathy only increase your distress by reminding you that you no longer have your loved one here.[8]

The person experiencing loss cannot believe that anyone knows exactly how he or she feels. Those who have been hurt by loss know these feelings well.

Preoccupation

The grieving person is absorbed with preoccupation of mind with the deceased person or the loved object. For the grieving it is difficult to think of anyone or anything else. The object or person remains focused in the mind of the grieving person. While friends and family members may attempt to move the person to other subjects and other things, the grieving person needs to talk about the deceased, about earlier memories and relationships, and about the pain brought about by the loss of the person. It is better to allow this lingering preoccupation than to attempt to evade it. It is far better for the grief-stricken individual to talk than to remain silent and withdrawn. However, the person's silence must be honored.

Inability to Carry Out Tasks

The grieving person demonstrates an inability to stick to one activity. He or she finds it hard to do anything with enthusiasm or for any long period. Although this would be expected in the early moments of grief, it sometimes lasts for days, weeks, and months. In the weeks that follow the death of a husband, a homemaker may find it difficult to stick to cleaning the house, washing the dishes, finishing a dress that has been cut out, or in engaging in other activities that formerly were meaningful. A husband whose wife has died will likely experience awkwardness, frustration, inefficiency in tasks, and lack of enthusiasm in his domestic responsibilities and in his vocational life. It becomes impossible to follow through on a chosen endeavor to successful conclusion.

Difficulty with Social Interaction

The grief sufferer has difficulty in interacting socially. Even though a grieving person may go through the motions of relating socially, it is very hard for him to put his heart into relating interpersonally. The depression a grieving person experiences can sometimes leave him with a sense of apathy toward life. Social contacts that previously have been meaningful simply do not have the same importance during the time of grief. His intense preoccupation with the loss experienced may cause him to close out friends or associates. The pastor encounters this in persons who have pursued a very active life in the church and community who, at the time of grief, cannot find energy for the discharge of their responsibilities or take part in meaningful church or community activities. It is often the pastor who can "run interference" for the grieving person by educating friends and church members to the normalcy of social withdrawal when grief occurs. Such intervention discourages others from exerting pressure on the grieving person to get back into an active, participating life before grief has run its course.

Loss of Meaning in One's Life

The grief sufferer feels that life has lost its meaning. The emotional energies invested in a loved person or a loved object are not quickly or easily given up, and the absence of the loved object or person leaves a huge void. In a real sense that relationship in his life has lost its meaning. The tendency at the time of loss is to lose perspective. The loss becomes ultimate and, in a sense, distorted. It is a tendency for the helping professional to superimpose meaningfulness. It is difficult for the minister to see the folly of trying to talk a person out of these feelings. Speaking of the grief emotions, Flynt (1967) says the following:

> There is a sense of unreality giving you the impression that you are living in another world. Everything looks the same, but it isn't. You busy yourself with your customary activities but your heart isn't in it, and you merely go through the motions. Sometimes you have difficulty arriving at a simple decision. Matters to which you would normally give an automatic response now seem to demand an inordinate amount of mental debate. There is an ache in your heart, a drabness to life, and an emptiness that seems unbearable. As one man expressed it, "My love for my wife had not changed. It is just the same as it has always been. What I miss so is her loving me in return!" This is an emotional void, and sometimes curious and strange indeed are the feelings that rush in and fill the vacuum.[9]

Sometimes the reaction to acute loss is utter despair. To the grief sufferer, life appears to have lost its meaning. Nothing seems to be worth the effort required to carry it out. To try to carry on without the love and companionship of the person who has died appears to be more of a burden than the mourner is willing or able to bear. "If this despair and anger turned against the person persists over a long period of time, life can settle into a state of depression."[10] Attempts to reconstruct meaning in the face of this feeling are usually doomed to failure. Time must be allowed for the person to do his own reconstructing.

Feelings of Anxiety

Both generalized anxiety and specific anxieties characterize the grieving person. The future looks bleak; he does not know what lies ahead. He knows only that he has been deprived of something precious. Specific anxieties arise out of uncertainty in carrying out the wishes of the deceased, of unresolved preferences for final disposition of the deceased, of arrangements for memorializing the deceased, and even questions surrounding details and future directions of the survivor's own life. The threat of one's own nonbeing produces anxiety. The first assertion about the nature of anxiety is this: anxiety is the state in which a being is aware of its possible nonbeing. The same statement, in its shorter form, would read: anxiety is the existential awareness of non-being.[11] This primal threat to existence has such deep roots that superficial assurances and pious words do not touch the depths of his grief. Patience and compassion are called for along with expertise in helping the grieving person to understand what is going on within.

COMMON REACTIONS AND RESPONSES IN GRIEF

Despite personality variations, there are a number of common reactions and responses which grief elicits. The reactions and responses listed here are descriptive but largely normative. However, as in the profile above it is impossible to categorize all grief sufferers.

Hostility

The first response that is usually encountered is hostility. Some persons become angry when they lose or misplace an object. Generally this anger is directed within for being so careless. If it be true that even minor losses occasion anger, how much more reasonable to believe that to lose something or someone permanently evokes much greater anger. Freud is reported to have said: "A grieving person is an angry person."

Many times loss in death is directed toward the physician or nurse, to the pastor, to neighbors, to family members, and toward God. When one loses a meaningful object or a person in death, the loss painfully reminds him of his own inability to control life. The frustration one has experienced produces anger. Sometimes the grieving person becomes angry at the deceased for having died. At other times he may become angry with God, who is sometimes blamed for having taken the person away. That God is sometimes the villain is demonstrated by the young father of two preschool children whose wife had died. In the grief process, he very strongly blurted out, "God, what do you mean by this?" Regina Flesch (1969) makes the point well: "The greatest obstacle to communication between the mourner and the sympathizer lies in the sympathizer's unpreparedness for the mourner's anger. Although a common part of the process, this anger is seldom, if ever, discussed openly."[12] Unless the pastor is careful he can fall into a practice of heaping shame upon the grieving person for expressing these deep feelings of anger. Especially vulnerable is the minister who feels that he needs to defend God against the anger of a bereaved family member. "If both mourner and sympathizer could accept that irrational hostility as a universal part of the mourning itself, the roles of both would become easier."[13]

Resignation

With some grief sufferers, resignation is a common response. The grieving person feels there is nothing that can be done as "this is God's will, so we will just have to accept it." Resignation is the only defense that some grief-stricken persons are able to muster. Initially, to some it is the only rational and emotional way to cope with death.

Guilt

Guilt is a very common response at the time of bereavement. There are hardly any grief situations in which there is not some guilt. This is not only common to the grief experience but to a wide range of life experiences which grief touches. Some of the most common ways in which guilt surfaces are the following:

Guilt Concerning Unrealized Ambitions for the Deceased

A man worked for wages for a number of years and then decided that he would like to start his own business. However, death intervened and the wife felt guilty for not having supported him. She may have discouraged his venture because of the uncertainty of income, economic risks, and nature of the business itself. His untimely death causes her to become consumed with guilt. Such circumstances make it difficult for her to deal with the guilt she feels.

Guilt Concerning Particular Relationships with the Deceased

Two brothers have been feuding for many years. One is killed or dies suddenly, and the surviving brother has intense feelings of guilt because of his own involvement in the faulty relationship. He is likely to blame himself for not having been a better brother or for not having remedied the relationship before it was too late. Similarly, the death of a spouse is almost certain to produce irrational guilt feelings since all spousal relationships are imperfect at best.

Guilt Concerning Certain Choices Made with Respect to Medical Care for the Deceased

Usually this occurs when family members blame themselves for not having chosen a different hospital, did not take the deceased to another physician, or did not follow through on some new drug that had been discovered. The guilt occasioned by the loss is then distorted or exaggerated out of proportion to the actual events surrounding the death of the deceased.

Guilt Concerning Relief About Not Having to Deal with the Deceased Person Again

This occurs because of ambivalent feelings which we have toward almost every person of our acquaintance. When we live in close contact with persons, we have mixed feelings about them. Individuals normally carry some feelings of love and hate at the same time. At times, a survivor feels inordinately guilty because he or she feels relief at the person's death. Consider the daughter or son whose mother has lived with the family for a good number of years. In declining health, she necessitated a lot of care on the part of the daughter or son and the other family members. Thus, the whole routine of the family has been disrupted, deprivations have occurred, and many adjustments have been made. Now that the mother has died, feelings of relief and guilt about feeling the relief have arisen. Younger family members who have had to curtail some of their activities on behalf of the grandmother now are free to pursue some of their own interests. They are relieved that they have more freedom, yet they realize that it is grandmother who has died and they feel guilty. Still another instance is that of the pastor who has been thwarted by a certain prominent member in his church. When that prominent and influential member dies, the pastor feels relief but then recognizes that this is culturally and immorally beneath him to feel this way. This results in an emotional "diverticulosis" in which the emotion of guilt telescopes back upon the emotion of relief and sets up a situation in which one feels caught. Assuagement of this guilt and relief may take considerable time.

A lot of the guilt in grief comes about because one both wants the loved person or object out of the way but also wants to hold on to him or her. Irrespective of the way in which this guilt arises or the character of the relationship which occasions the guilt, it is nevertheless a real factor which we have to recognize and deal with.

Guilt the Survivor Feels at Being the Survivor

Survivors older than the deceased person are the most likely candidates for this manifestation of guilt. An elderly parent questions why he or she could not have died in place of the son or daughter.

One must make distinctions in the proper consideration of the guilt occasioned by grief. It is quite essential that we recognize that guilt is normal at the time of grief. The grief sufferer is prone to wonder what he could have done to have prevented the loss of the person or the object. He becomes entangled emotionally with his own responsibility in the loss sustained. The surviving spouse of a suicidal person asks himself or herself, "What could I have done to prevent this?" Our involvements as persons are such that there is reality to our feelings of responsibility. It is important to make some clear-cut distinctions about guilt. Guilt, whether connected to grief or not, is quite often disproportionate to the facts themselves. Normal guilt is appropriate to the facts of separation or death; abnormal guilt becomes morbid, characterized by inordinate length, behavioral manifestation, and obsessive resistance to acceptance of the loss.

A sound pastoral approach and safe rule-of-thumb is the working knowledge that abnormal guilt is differentiated from normal guilt by matter or the degree as well as by its duration. Dealing with guilt appropriately may keep the grief sufferer from experiencing severe emotional problems. True or normal guilt refers to failure and sin where the person knows that he has done wrong and he feels an appropriate sense of guilt. False guilt has little or no factual basis. More properly the concern is shame, not guilt. Shame enters when one is faced with the expectations of others or when one's superego introjects irrational prohibitions present in one's culture. The sense of shame and guilt becomes exaggerated out of proportion. Group standards or religious ideas are determined by either the group or the religious community to which one belongs. False and unrealistic guilt surfaces in those persons who feel guilty over angry feelings they have had at times at their parents or toward their relatives, angry feelings that are reality based but for which the person has inordinate guilt. These feelings are accentuated at death or loss. Nuland (1994) observes correctly, "When we mourn, it should be the loss of love that makes us grieve, not the guilt that we did something wrong."[14]

Important to remember in exercising responsible pastoral care is the necessity for taking quite seriously guilt feelings, whether these are real or imaginary, true or false. These must be faced since emotions are always at the raw edge. During the time of grief many of our feelings of guilt are distorted out of proportion to prevailing facts. Dealing with guilt in the bereaved person takes patience, time, understanding, and love. Judgment and premature reassurances are inappropriate and nonproductive. In the immediate moment of grief it is better to simply allow the grief sufferer to verbalize his feelings of guilt, and deal with these later in subsequent pastoral conversations. When feelings of guilt are being revealed it is important for the pastor to note these in his own mind, so that he can return to them later in conversation with the grieving person. He should be alert to the signals that are being given out at this time. When the pastor identifies morbid guilt in the survivor, wisdom may mandate a referral to the appropriate resource of grief counselor, psychologist, or psychiatrist. The pastor's time constraints and lack of expertise in grief work may make this his most responsible course of action.

Suppressed Feelings

A grieving person commonly keeps feelings under tight control. In an attempt to be brave he puts up false fronts. Feelings are buried beneath the surface and are not allowed expression. Sensitive to the scrutiny of others, the grieving person conceals his true feelings and emotional states, especially during prefuneral arrangements and the service itself. In religious guise the grief sufferer sometimes may say, "I know I have my faith which enables me to accept this." Culture and religion impose an unfair burden on the grieving person when it is expected that he show stability and faith by being unemotional during and following memorial services. A grieving person who suppresses his grief may be surrendering to culture demands, group mores, or community expectations. This person may tend to delay or even to deny the grief reaction or to observe the death in an unrealistic way. Not giving in to emotion could be misinterpreted as lacking faith in God. Internally the experience may be disturbing and difficult. He will not let go because someone might think him un-Christian or unholy. Unless the pastor is careful, he may give cues which might suggest that expressing grief is un-Christian, that somehow the griever, being more than human, is supposed to rise above this transitory existence.[15] While suppressed feelings have the value of keeping the person from going through panic or hysterical reaction, suppression may often be a cover for true feelings. In dealing therapeutically with grief, however, the feelings must be allowed to come out at some time. It is healthier to deal with grief by expressing, rather than controlling, one's feelings.

> Your grief will be eased if you can express your feelings. If you want to cry, then cry. If you want to protest against the injustice of life, do so. It is better to let your feelings go than to bury them deep, where they can fester or eat away at you. Face the full pain of your loss, for your pain is not only deep—it is healthy. It means that you are alive. That is why it is not a

humane act to give sedatives to relieve the acute edge of suffering. To give temporary relief from pain and thereby to prolong
its effects is not a kindness. It is easier to deal with the effects
when people around you are aware of what is happening and
why. Months later, the delayed reactions will not be as clearly
understood or as sympathetically handled by the bereaved person or those around him.[16]

Constant Activity

The grieving person is likely to engage in feverish activity. The
person seeks to lose himself in activities and work in order to take
his mind off the grief experience. In the initial shock period of grief,
this may not be obvious. In the days immediately following the loss,
however, the person may go from one thing to another and to engage
in certain chores that have been temporarily laid aside. The grieving
person who is unemployed may seek employment, believing this
may help. There is a time in grief work when finding an activity or
work with meaning is necessary. This should come later as the grief
sufferer attempts to engage in new patterns of behavior and productive work as a way of rechanneling affections and drives.

Refusal to Let Go

A grieving person often engages in refusal to let the deceased
person go. The trauma of shock and radical nature of personal loss
in death commonly causes the grief sufferer to hold on to the
deceased. Dealing with this difficulty requires skillful pastoral care.
Helping a survivor to let go of the deceased person demands
patience. It is with reluctance that any one of us gives up something
that is precious and dear to him. This reluctance can be seen when a
surviving spouse has difficulty clearing dresser drawers, closets,
and the little nooks and crannies in which the deceased has kept
personal belongings. It is painful to dispose of personal effects. The
survivor will want to keep these possessions where the deceased left
them. The wife may leave the husband's shotgun or fishing rod in
his favorite corner of the room. A reasonable time lapse is good
because of the adjustment that the survivor is attempting to make to

the loss of the deceased. It can, however, become a morbid grief response if it is drawn out over an inordinate length of time, or if the survivor still insists on doing such things as setting a place at the dinner table for the deceased. There does come a time, however, when true release is obtained, characterized by a surviving wife who confided to a counselor, "I am so glad to have that casket removed from around my neck."

Jackson (1964) observes, "One of the psychological facts we have to cope with is the heavy investment of emotional capital in the objects we come to love, and the need to withdraw that emotional capital when there is no longer a possibility for a significant human relationship."[17] Even though the pain is real, ". . . it is released more quickly if it is more openly faced for what it is. It is prolonged endlessly if ignored or denied. We must learn to respect our deep feelings and the deep feelings of others, and to create the channels through which these valid feelings can be wisely expressed."[18]

Denial

Denial is one of the most pronounced responses. Denial is the reluctance of the bereaved person to admit the loss at all. Time is a very critical and essential element for dealing with pronounced denial. The impact of denial is shown in an experience which a hospital chaplain had when a middle-aged father was killed on his way home from work. He was dead on arrival at the hospital emergency room and the chaplain was called in to minister to the distraught wife and son. The mother could not believe it. After talking for a few minutes, even though she was told that her husband was dead, she wanted to get details over with so that she and her son could go home. She said, "I know he will be coming home and we must go home and get his supper ready." So strong was her denial that she could not believe her husband was dead. Reality came only after the hospital chaplain told her that the husband would not come home tonight, that he would never come home again in the same way, and that he was dead. The chaplain also said, "Tonight is real; you are not dreaming. This is the place where they brought him after he died in an accident. I only wish things could be the way that they used to be; we all wish that. But things will never be exactly the same again. I am sorry, but your husband is dead and you are going home to an empty house." The wife was able to understand. It was then that she broke down and cried. It was only then that she shed tears for the first time. Without doubt there were many months and days that followed during which she could not believe the truth of her husband's death.

Social Withdrawal

The grief-stricken person will often withdraw from social contacts. He will not be interested in going to church or synagogue, take part in social activities, will absent himself from clubs, or will not be able to go to work for a period of time. It is natural to withdraw from social contacts which are reminders of the life lived by the person who has died or the object that is lost. Often very religious persons who have been quite active in church activities, and leaders in the church life, will not be present to take their accustomed responsibilities at church. On occasion church members who have admired that strong faith of the grief sufferer may become critical. To these friends it appears that if the person would come back to church or community life and become active again, he would be better able to deal with the loss. Although this sounds good in theory, it is artificial and unrealistic. Social contacts are difficult for a person in grief. The griever needs time to ease back into those social and religious streams which characterized his life before his loss.

Sympathetic Symptoms

In the days which follow the initial shock of grief, it is sometimes customary for the grief sufferer to attempt to extend the deceased in his own person. The grieving person may take on and experience some of the physical symptoms which characterized the deceased person in the later stages of his illness. A person whose mother or father met death through a heart attack may have sympathetic pains in somewhat the same way that husbands of pregnant wives report that they too experience labor pains. Another common manifestation of this extension comes through mannerisms practiced by the survivor that were a part of the life of the deceased. Voice inflections, gestures, idiosyncrasies, and lifestyles may be adopted by the survivor. Another way in which the person is extended in the survivor occurs when the survivor takes up and follows the occupation of the deceased. The wife whose husband had an insurance or realty business may attempt to carry on the business in the name of her deceased husband. In our modern culture it is often mandated that a wife continue her husband's business for financial survival. She should be clear in her own mind about her needs and motivation. The son of a minister or a physician often may feel that the father's mantle is placed upon him at death and he will seek to become a minister or a physician in order to carry forward the unfinished work of a father.

Physical Symptoms

There is evidence to believe that some grieving persons take on unconsciously based physical symptoms. A number of physicians contend that some psychosomatic illnesses have roots in unresolved grief. This is not always true. Nevertheless it is thought by some that asthma, arthritis, dermatological problems, and musculoskeletal abnormalities are results of repressed grief. Add to this hypertension and anxiety which have roots in an unresolved grief. There is good reason to believe that some respiratory, dermatological, and cardiovascular disorders have an etiology in grief that has been repressed. It is safe to believe that normal grief usually includes somatic distress. Anxiety states affect the cardiovascular functions of one's body.

Depression

The grief sufferer experiences depressiveness or depressed states. These feelings almost always occur in normal grief reactions. Though they may differ in degree and in duration, they are present at one point or another in the grief sufferer's experience. As others observe the grief sufferer, the depression is a mood which comes over a person bringing with it feelings of rejection and gloom. It is characterized by the slowing down of bodily activity and feelings of guilt and worthlessness. Commonly the depressed person's head will hang down, his body will slouch, he will talk in a monotone, and will often talk of gloomy, negative thoughts and subjects. He tends to avoid company and will have a depressing effect upon those he meets. This can denote a loss of self-esteem caused by a breakdown, a frustration, or a loss of an interpersonal relationship.

The grief sufferer who expresses depressive feelings generally suffers simple depression from which he may be able to recover. He could need the help of others as he resolves his depression. In a simple depression one is generally agitated, anxious, and upset. He is reacting to his acute loss and is reacting normally. This condition is sometimes known as situational depression, because the trauma of the situation brings depressed feelings. The depressed person is likely to feel discouraged, and may experience guilt. Most persons suffer simple depression at one time or another arising out of life's experiences. The student who fails in his grades in school, the businessman who does not achieve the goal in business that he has set for himself, the coach who has a losing season in sports, a married couple experiencing interpersonal conflict, and persons who fail to get along with others with whom they work, are situations that bring depressed feelings. To call this a simple depression is not to say that it is resolved simply. It takes time and determination for depression to be resolved.

Simple depression is vastly different from acute depression or a depressive stupor, both of which are much more deep-seated. Depression resulting from a death or a loss needs to be taken seriously or the depression may worsen. It is important to allow the person with depressed feelings to ventilate the feelings he is experiencing and for others to take his loss seriously.

Acute depression is much more serious in nature; it can also result from the loss of a person or an object. In acute depression the person is often much more despondent and in some cases is even desperate. He shows little initiative, speaks only after long pauses, is not interested in activities, and has very little energy. At times he may pace the floor or weep a great deal. Many of these manifestations are experienced by the grief sufferer. In dealing with grieving persons we are likely to find more persons suffering from acute depression than from simple depression. The acutely depressed person needs more care, attention, and realistic compassion. It takes longer for him to pull out of his depression than one who is suffering a mild depression.

Depression and depressiveness can be detected conversationally. The bereaved person's preoccupation with morbid talk of meaningless existence without the deceased is a sure sign of depression. Excessive consumption of alcohol or drugs indicates a depression that is unmanageable without these helps. Melancholia and withdrawal from social contacts may also give the helper a clue to depressiveness in the bereaved. In some cases psychiatric help is necessary to enable the bereaved to deal with his depression.

Another condition which the griever may experience is depressive stupor. This person may even become motionless and unresponsive. He is so preoccupied with thoughts of guilt and punishment that he cannot get on with living. It is possible that this person's mood may lead to thoughts of self-destruction. When one person loses another it is not unusual for thoughts and feelings of suicide to enter and absorb the mind. Taking up life again becomes so difficult for some that suicide is felt to be the only way out of their misery. In this case the grief sufferer should be referred to a psychiatrist with both minister and psychiatrist working together to bring healing. It must be strongly emphasized that the person in a depressive stupor needs the kind of medical help which pastors are unable to give. Whenever the pastor attempts to deal with such a person it must be in consultation with a psychiatrist as prescription medication may be needed. Other treatment may be indicated, including hospitalization.

Since the pastor is often the professional person closest to the grief sufferer, he should acquaint himself with the symptomatology of depression. He should be well acquainted with a psychiatrist and other professionals to whom referral can be made when indicated. At the base of depressiveness there is a close connection between depression and loss or disruption of a relationship. Some common symptoms of depression are aggressive tendencies, denial, guilt, rhythmic mood swings, early waking, psychosomatic ailments such as headaches and stomach pains, stooped posture, avoidance of food, and disinterest in sexual activities. Family members can help the minister by letting him know about these emotional and physical symptoms. It is good to remember that some of the causes of depression might involve marital maladjustment, death in the person's family, childbirth, a person's physical condition, economic stress, and disappointment caused by failure to achieve certain personal goals.

Dependency

Expression of dependency is characteristic in the grieving person's emotional symptomatology. Those who experience loss through separation or death often become abnormally dependent upon others. Sometimes this dependency is expressed in overt physical ways: simple leaning on someone else to cry, wanting someone else to do something that they are capable of doing themselves, or making what might appear to be excessive and unreasonable requests of those who offer help. It is difficult not to indulge the grief sufferer. It is not uncommon for dependency needs to take the form of manipulative behavior when one is in grief. Regressive patterns of behavior that border on the infantile may surface. Whenever extreme crisis threatens a person, he reverts to previous behavior that worked for him at an earlier time. It can be expected that the grief-stricken person may consciously or unconsciously contrive to exploit the friendly overtures of concerned persons and may often take advantage of their well-intentioned gestures of sympathy and support. It is always good to recognize this for what it is and to be somewhat indulgent with the grief sufferer during the initial phases of his grief reaction as long as this indulgence does not become habitual or unreasonable.

Compensatory Reactions

The grief sufferer is likely to engage in compensatory reactions. This is true of parents who are standing by the bedside of a dying child, or sons and daughters standing by and witnessing the death of a father or mother. Anticipating the coming death and under the guise of being kind parents to their child, parents may compensate for many of their feelings of guilt, regret, or failure. They may tend to indulge the patient with special favors, for example, food, luxurious items, excessive gifts, or additional pain medications administered to the patient. It is good to remember that these may be temporary stop-gap measures to compensate for guilt feelings on the part of the concerned family.

These responses suggest considerable variety in the ways that people meet the distresses of grief, and indicate that almost any kind of emotional response can be expected from a grieving person.

These responses also suggest the importance of dealing constructively with grief. A. H. Kutscher (1971) has observed that bereavement can be looked at as an illness.

> The bereaved may be regarded as a patient with a definite complex of symptoms, often sub-clinical, which may become exacerbated, severe, and even fatal. . . . The bereaved, as a patient, requires treatment, especially in the early stages, to prevent any more serious progression. Unfortunately, our culture tends to ignore the fact that the problems with loss and grief do not begin at the moment of the loved one's death and that there is much anticipatory grief that follows notification of the patient's unfavorable prognosis.[19]

I contend that in grief the whole of one's being is diseased. Descriptively, disease is a state in which health becomes illness. In the grief sufferer the diseased state is more predominant that the healthy state. I contend that grief is a disease.

Proper treatment of grief is important both before a terminal patient dies and for survivors after death has occurred if emotional and physical problems more severe and more profound are to be avoided. Proper treatment consistent with sound emotional and spiritual insights can help grieving persons to recover from grief, readjust to life, find new hope, and to experience meaningful life again. Certain myths still persist, irrespective of upbringing and culture. They are common, as James and Cherry (1989) suggest: ". . . bury your feelings, replace the loss, grieve alone, just give it time, regret the past, don't trust."[20] All of these are bad advice, false, and harmful. And our environment/culture places dozens of others upon us.

HEALTHY MANAGEMENT OF GRIEF

Several pertinent factors are important in dealing effectively with the grief sufferer. *Grief management is always slow.* Interactions and interrelationships the grief sufferer had with the deceased cause the roots of emotional attachment to run deep. For the pastor who is dealing with the grief sufferer, it is sometimes impossible to decipher accurately the strength of these emotional attachments. These are often deeper than is realized. Emotions are intricate and complex in nature, and the forces of love and hate are among the strongest feelings in human nature. The grief sufferer may be caught up in a vortex of strong feelings and mixed feelings. Grief brings almost every emotion that persons are capable of experiencing. The process of dealing with profound grief is exceedingly tedious and painfully slow.

Counselors and pastors are often asked, "How long does grief work take?" Some suggest that a period of six to eighteen months is a necessary time span for dealing with grief. There are varying opinions about length of time. At least a year's time is necessary for wholesome grief work and the beginning and partial resolution of grief. In a year's time the complete circuit of significant days and events are experienced. Christmas, Easter, Thanksgiving, Passover, Hanukkah, birthdays, anniversaries, children's birthdays, or other special days or occasions which have become family rituals are revisited and experienced afresh as these come and go. In *From Beginning to End*[21] Robert Fulghum (1995) emphasizes what many have known and practiced for many years—that there are many rituals of our lives. As his title suggests, these significant rituals relate not only to our living, but to our dying as well. It is at these special times particular feelings are likely to surface again and memories return to remind a grieving person of experiences he had shared with the deceased.

From beginning to end,
the rituals of our lives shape each hour, day, and year.
Everyone leads a ritualized life:
Rituals are repeated patterns of meaningful acts.
If you are mindful of your actions, you will see the ritual patterns.
If you see the patterns, you may understand them.
If you understand them, you may enrich them.
In this way, the habits of a lifetime become sacred.

Is this so?[22]

With many persons it takes even longer than a year's time, depending upon the nature of the relationship, the personhood of the bereaved, the support systems utilized, and the manner in which the grief experience is managed. Once grief is honestly faced and satisfactorily managed, emotional scars remain and memories linger.

The minister working with the bereaved must avoid the temptation to attempt to take care of the grief sufferer in a short time or an expected time frame. It is a mistake to believe that grief can be managed quickly; it takes time and patience for a person to get over his grief. Often we have heard it said that time heals everything, but this is not so—it is what happens and what is done in time that helps the griever to heal.

Kutscher (1970/1971) says,

> Time does heal some of us in time, in and of itself; we are not denying that. . . . we must take the time concept further and insist that it is what the bereaved *does* and *accomplishes* with this time, which determines how long it will take one to heal and how successful the healing will be.[23]

It takes time to experience healing, and it is different for each person. During the days and weeks immediately following the death of a family member or another grief-inducing experience, it is good for the minister to make frequent, short visits. This helps to deepen the relationship for further, more intensive grief work in the weeks to follow. Although frequent visits soon after the loss is sustained are important, the minister needs to be functionally available and present to grieving persons whenever that person announces a need. He will find it important to continue to be alert to whatever signals may be coming from this person. The work of the pastor calls for flexibility sufficient to allow the person to talk briefly or at some length about the feelings occasioned by death or loss. The pastor needs to be available when these occasions arise. The grief process can never be programmed, nor can it be superficially treated.

Reality

Grief management must take reality into account. The separation must be faced realistically and the affections rechanneled. Beliefs about life after death sometimes lead the bereaved and the community to follow somewhat questionable theological ideas. Perhaps we err greatest in the choice of epitaphs for grave markers. The poetic aphorisms "He is not dead but sleepeth," "He is only resting," "Here lies 'John Jones,' he sleeps in Jesus," or "Here lies 'Susie,' she has gone away for a little while" may give some measure of consolation to the grieving family, but they tell only a partial story so far as reality is concerned. Harsh and cruel as death may be, it is irreversible. With respect to life in this present world, the person is dead, never to live again in the same way. Never again will he walk this earth. This is a reality to be faced. Certain funeral customs and faulty cultural ideas sometimes serve to confuse the emotional and spiritual settling of death's reality. In wholesome grief management the reality of death must be taken seriously and acknowledged by survivors.

Freedom

The grief-stricken person must become free from the loved person or the loved object. In grief one never becomes totally free from the memory of the deceased person or object. Nonetheless, one must be freed from the unreality of supposing that life can and will be the same again. Cliches, aphorisms, and metaphors such as "sleeping" and "gone away" are likely to confuse and complicate, as does our sophistocated substitution of "expired" for "died." This is true with children who are told that "mother has gone to be with Jesus and will be away for a little while." The curious and inquisitive child is puzzled by this kind of talk and lives with the anticipation that in a few weeks mother may be back. The important point is that the grieving person must acknowledge that the loss has actually occurred. A part of this is acceptance that the broken bond is real and that the relationship will never be the same as it was before. It is difficult yet necessary.

Idealization

Grief management involves idealization. Idealization as I define it is the emotional experience of sorting out the nature of the relationship that has existed between the deceased and the survivor. It means taking seriously the positive and the negative, the good and not so good. Emotional and relational clarities and ambiguities do surface with death, if survivors, friends, and pastor are frank. Facing these honestly is accompanied by verbal and emotional expression. The beginnings of the idealization process occur as families gather, as friends reach out to comfort, and as the funeral is observed by survivors. Idealization in grief may properly begin with spoken remembrances of ideals, values, and virtues of the deceased but does not end there. As admirable qualities of the deceased are remembered, other lesser admired qualities also surface and are remembered. I hold "idealization" in grief from the root, "idea," to be both the good and the not so good. Ideas partake of both. It is important that both be allowed expression for perspective to be gained by grieving persons. When the expression is not rooted in reality, the grieving person disbelieves it and may fantasize unrealistically. The danger of idealization lies in the tendency of the grieving person, friends, and pastor to misrepresent reality and to attribute nonexistent qualities to the deceased. It is helpful in grief work for honest dialogue about the person to occur. No matter how questionable the character or morals of the person may be, it is generally true that good qualities and attributes were a part of his or her life. The converse is true also. It is helpful to remember these good qualities in the process of idealization because such remembrances help to ease the pain. When the grieving person idealizes, he frequently begins with the positive aspects of the relationship. In time idealization of good qualities gives way to reality assessment. This makes it possible for the grieving person to focus and to verbalize the negative aspects of the life of the deceased. It enables him to see the deceased in the true sense of that life. There is hardly any person one can imagine but with whom it was not in some sense good to know and good to have some relationship. The Christian gospel is often quite helpful at this point because in the ministry of Jesus he was far more concerned with the person's motivations than with outward behavior. Persons whose lifestyle may have been questionable can be seen also to have had noble motivations within.

Acceptance of Pain

Acceptance of emotional and spiritual pain is necessary to healthy grief management. Acceptance of pain is healthy. Pain felt and expressed by talking and weeping is diminished and clears the way for other facets of reality adjustment. No grieving person should be deprived of the opportunity to express pain of body, mind, spirit, and emotions. Expressions of pain are often uncomfortable for those who sit by and watch. It is disconcerting to see someone tormented by the painful memories that a loss occasions. Nevertheless, it is of utmost importance that this pain be endured, lived through, accepted, and believed. The pastor must resist the temptation to cover up pain prematurely by smoothly couched words and urbane cliches. To see someone in extreme emotional, physical, or mental distress tempts a pastor to rush in to ease the pain. The temptation is strong for ministers to hasten to the rescue and to attempt to cushion the blow emotionally and spiritually. This is a disservice to the bereaved. Pain temporarily and prematurely alleviated likely will surface later in more profound disturbances than the initial pain would have occasioned. In making the adjustment to grief, as the days lengthen into weeks and years, deep wounds slowly begin to heal. "Life will never again be quite the same as it was, but there is still life to be lived and it still can be good."[24]

New Relationships

The formation of new relationships and interests aids the bereaved person in adjusting to the loss of the former relationship. It is essential that the grieving person develop new friends and new patterns of life. This important facet of grief work depends largely upon the readiness of the bereaved person. There is no great rush to move the grief sufferer to form new relationships. Time is itself important, and one should be allowed to move at his own speed. The therapeutic use of this time involves the reshuffling of old thoughts, introduction of new thoughts and plans, the exploration of new trails and company of old and new friends, a process of weaving the old life with a new one; immersing oneself in all of life's interests, activities, and responsibilities.[25]

Nevertheless, in due time one needs encouragement to venture into new endeavors of a personal and interpersonal nature. Kutscher (1969) suggests that among some of the ways of redirecting the energies of one's self and rechanneling affections and emotional responses can come about through diversions such as reading,

music, sports, travel, hobbies, companionship, remarriage, and varied forms of entertainment.[26] Additionally, the investment of one's
self in a variety of caring opportunities for someone else and for the
preparation of the greater good of mankind is helpful. For some this
may come to focus through a career, social action, religious work,
social activities, or the pursuit of ambitions formerly denied to the
survivor. Whatever pursuits or activities that challenge the personal
resources and talents of the survivor would likely lead into fulfill-
ments and satisfactions that give new depths of meaning to his
emerging personhood. Much of the strength of *Death and Bereavement*,[27] edited by Kutscher, lies in the help it offers at the points of
the psychosocial implications of loss in grief and the direction to be
taken by the bereaved to achieve satisfactory physical and emotional
recovery and to enable a person to live once again. Depending upon
the age of the person, this new relationship may indeed be the
development of an intimate relationship with someone near the
same age as the grief sufferer. There is no reason, psychologically or
religiously, why a person who loses his spouse in the early, mid, or
late years of his life should not marry again for whatever legitimate
motivations seem to be present should this be desired. For some this
would be reinvesting emotional capital into and with another person. When one loses a spouse in marriage, life does not need to end.
Life for the remaining spouse will be difficult. At the moment of
separation by death some persons may fear that life will be very
much the same as formerly. In reality it cannot be. If one chooses
not to remarry, life will be different structurally and emotionally. If
one remarries, he or she is faced with relating to a person uniquely
different from the one to whom he or she was formerly related. But
this can become rewarding and fulfilling to the bereaved and to the
new person who becomes a part of the relationship.

Some spouses are reluctant to remarry because they feel that it is
a betrayal of the deceased. If a couple has discussed this possibility
before death strikes one or the other, guilt is alleviated and a wholesome adjustment to life can be made. "An important part of the
process of working through the grief is that of withdrawing the
emotional capital invested in the deceased and reinvesting it in the
relationship that can continue to bear fruit in life."[28]

Because the grief experience reaches deeply into the emotional structure of the individual, it is important that the activities engage him at the time of his bereavement and encourage a firm grip on reality rather than a flight into fantasy. For some, the escape into the unreal with narcotics for the body, sedation for the emotions, and the fanciful philosophy for the mind are already too much of a possibility. So, the religious practices that are employed should fortify reality rather than deny it.[29]

Grief that is not resolved will continue to plague a person, hinder worthwhile and needed relationships, and erode vitality. There is no escaping persisting pain and suffering. Gaining a new identity, a transformation, is essential to grief recovery. Important steps include adjustment to the loss, determination to keep on living productively, reframing of lifestyle, acting for the good of oneself, and hoping for better days. These steps help us to face the loss, be renewed, and reinvigorated. Spoken pastorally, Clemons (1994) suggests: "Say hello to grief work, say goodbye to your loss, say hello to God, say hello to your future."[30]

Whatever adjustments are made, whatever activities are encouraged, whatever options are chosen, these should be realistically assessed and carefully considered with respect to the person's perception of himself. One's self-perceptions become more valid if he weighs these with someone other than himself and those closest to him.

Perhaps the most important pastoral ministry one can give is emotional presence, attentive and listening ears, spiritual support, and assurance of continuing support and prayers. In a practical way one can provide a sanctuary of privacy, a place of retreat, an environment of safety, and a presence of calmness and stability.

Chapter 5

The Value and Utilization
of Religious Resources

Pastors and those engaged in specialized ministries of pastoral care and counseling conceive their genius and power to lie in resources beyond themselves and above the dying and grieving. The minister functions from the faith that there is a power that transcends human finiteness—the power of God. Jackson (1964) states the following:

> The major religions of mankind have helped the grief-stricken face the emotional crises of life. They have done it by meeting three needs: the need for perspective in life; the need for spiritual values in measuring life; and the need for inner strength on the part of the bereaved person.[1]

The minister believes that such resources have their ultimate origin in God. In his calling he seeks to embody these resources and to give proclamation to these resources. What are these resources and how are they offered?

THE MINISTER'S ROLE

"Perhaps we may say that the minister in the hospital is a symbolic figure, a man who represents God, makes God present . . . the minister must be prepared not to fall back on traditional form but to try simply *to be there*, to show his solidarity with man in his sickness."[2] This role is not confined to institutional context. A minister's presence in the time of grief calls forth a wide variety of religious responses. By virtue of their particular rearing, conditioning, background, and atmosphere of earlier life, persons will respond negatively or positively to a minister. The minister recognizes that there are a number of ways in which persons image him, and considerably influences the way they respond to his role.

Edgar Jackson (1959) says the following:

> Modern psychological understanding verifies the value of religious rites, rituals, and practices which, and through anthropological studies have found, were long practiced in fortifying the individual against the stress of grief and during the work of mourning. These grief practices have developed out of the need to serve the full spectrum of mental life, and what is interpreted as racial and superstitious at the conscious level is often satisfying a deeper need of the being beyond the normal bounds of conscious mental activity. So it is, that the religious approach to the personality during the time of stress due to bereavement is concerned with depth and heights as well as breadth of understanding in dealing with the feelings of the individual. . . . The innate wisdom of religious practices seems to be not so much a matter of conscious design as of unconscious evaluation. The benefits of these practices are not determined adequately by relational judgment alone, but demand rather an understanding of the response of the emotions and spiritual sensitivities of the whole being.[3]

These images generally grow out of prior perceptions and misconceptions of one's ideas of a minister. They may also reflect the grief sufferer's ideas about the nature of God. Some of the more negative connotations associated with the minister can be understood through several suggestive images.

The minister is often regarded as a moral policeman. From this viewpoint he is seen as one who judges and condemns. He is seen as one whose function is to make moral pronouncements and to set standards for conduct and behavior. Dynamics of grief being what they are, the grief sufferer who has this limited understanding of a minister is quite often likely to feel guilt-ridden at the very presence of the minister.

The minister is sometimes seen as a dispenser of special favors. He may hear the request, "Pray for me, preacher, I need it." Conceived in this way the person in grief may look to the minister as one whose prayers are more efficacious than those of the grieving person. The grieving person may feel estrangement, guilt, or unworthiness before God. He may want the minister to plead his case before God.

It is not unusual for the dying or grieving person to see the minister as a "diviner" of unique mysteries. He is imaged as one in possession of deep spiritual mysteries unknown to other believers or professionals. Religious persons place the minister in the awesome position of having unusual spiritual perception. He is expected to be able to provide a special meaning or interpretation to dying or grieving persons of the hurtful events and of death. Although questions posed may seem strange, they should be considered seriously.

It is not uncommon for the minister to be regarded as prosecutioner for sins and misdeeds. He becomes one who determines punishment for the sufferer of guilt feelings. This sometimes happens through judgmental words in conversation or in prayers offered. Persons other than the minister contribute to judgmental attitudes. A physician known to the author created guilt within a husband and wife whose child had died when he told them that God was taking their child to show them they needed to "accept Christ as their Savior." The author was incensed. This sentiment of the physician was thoughtless and insensitive. One should bring spiritual pain to the grief sufferer. Many ministers are judgmental on other occasions and thus the dying and grieving may expect them to respond this way in grief situations. Some patients fear ministers because they have experienced a pastor who has been a prosecutioner.

THE SCRIPTURES

The Scriptures are another religious resource for the pastor's ministry to the grief sufferer. Few would argue against the use of the Scriptures as spiritual resources at the time of grief. It is not the use or nonuse of the Scriptures but the manner in which the Scriptures are used that is of critical concern. One approach employed by ministers at the time of grief is the *penal* use of the Scriptures. It is only judgment that is brought to bear upon the person. Some ministers believe that death is a propitious occasion for warning the survivors that they should prepare to meet God. They see a person's death as evidence that God is taking the family member in order to show others that they should make spiritual provision to die and to face the Day of Judgment. Authoritarian pronouncements from a pastor in such times of crisis provoke deep-seated guilt within the grief sufferer.

Survivors sometimes feel that the deceased was in some sense an atonement offering for their spiritual rebellion and negligence. Funeral sermons prepared and delivered for evangelistic reasons and to warn mourners of God's displeasure with their lives should be resisted. Feeling this is the only available opportunity for proclaiming the call to godly living and repentance, pastors sometimes use this occasion for such proposes.

The preferred approach is to use the Scriptures *pastorally.* In using the Scriptures pastorally the minister can help the person face himself and God. He then finds the Scriptures a source of direction toward emotional and spiritual salvation in both temporal and eschatological dimensions. When the Scriptures are used pastorally there is comfort and solace. The grief sufferer comes to feel that the eternal and ancient word is speaking to his present situation. He is brought to the recognition that this experience is not the end of life for him or for those whom he loves. Used pastorally the Scriptures become to him a stabilizing foundation upon which the mourner can attain perspective on ultimate issues of life.

The pastoral use is preferable in the grief situation; the question then becomes, "How do we use the Scriptures pastorally?"

The Scriptures Should Be Used Prescriptively

Prescriptive use of Scriptures means only the use of verses appropriate to the situation. The Scriptures abound in verses that offer comfort and assurance: "Blessed are those who mourn, for they shall receive comfort;" "I will never leave you nor forsake you;" "Lo, I am with you always;" "Be of good cheer, I have overcome the world;" "Nothing can separate us from the love of God which is in Christ Jesus." The repertoire of the minister's own personal knowledge, experience, and training enable him to add many more. Those Scriptures that have had personal meaning to the one who speaks the word of God at the time of crisis and bereavement have value and relevance.

The Scriptures Should Be Used Sparingly

Brief, related Scriptures have more meaning than lengthy passages, whether spoken or read. The time of grief is never a time for the minister to demonstrate his knowledge by quoting lengthy passages of Scripture from memory. Even though one may have memorized the Twenty-third Psalm, it is sometimes better to use one or two verses than to recite the entire Psalm in ministering to the grief-stricken. The same can be said for the Scriptures used during the funeral or memorial service. Using an economy of words in Scripture is made necessary by the short attention span of persons in grief. Well-chosen Scriptures carry more spiritual and emotional impact upon the grief sufferer than lengthy passages.

The Scriptures Should Be Used Contextually

Scriptures used should speak to the person in the context of his own struggle. It is more helpful to speak meaningfully to the needs of the sufferer than to meet one's own needs by exhaustive recitations or readings. Many of the Psalms reflect the intense personal struggles through which various persons have attempted to grapple with the deep issues of life, but use of many would be out of place in times of grief. Another limitless source of help are those verses of Scripture that reflect Paul's variety of experiences. Among these would the eighth chapter of Romans, Paul's theology of history, ending in the great hymn of praise in the latter part of the chapter in which he gives expression to his conviction that "nothing can separate us from the love of God which is in Christ Jesus." Assurances about the meaningfulness of life in God are a vital part of the historical record of the life of Jesus and are meaningful to grief sufferers (John 14; passages in the Corinthian epistles, among others).

The Scriptures Should Be Used Verbally

Appropriately chosen Scriptures spoken from memory to the grief sufferer convey comfort and understanding. Effectiveness is sometimes lost when the pastor reads long passages from the Bible in preference to simple, brief, easily remembered verses. There are occasions, however, when a family requests that the pastor read from the Scriptures, and this is appropriate and called for on occasion.

Even though the Scriptures are an important resource and a reminder of the presence of God, one need not feel compelled to read the Bible each time he makes contact with the grief sufferer. Wisdom would indicate that it depends upon where the person is in his spiritual struggle.

The minister will encounter persons who are nominally religious or antireligious. These sufferers are persons, too. The minister who incarnates the spirit of the Scriptures in his own personhood will be far more effective with these persons than he might otherwise be. Should he feel the need to leave a scriptural text with the nonreligious person, the exercise of such option could close the door to a meaningful ministry to such a person. As our society becomes more and more pluralistic in outlook, indications are that taking a person's feelings seriously, whatever be his religious orientation and at whatever point he may be spiritually, can open doors to significant future experiences of ministry. To take a person seriously at his own point of development or lack of it results in an effective witness. Since grief is of long duration, it is important to relate to the person from his point of view if our ministry is to have enduring value.

PRAYER

Prayer is another resource for the dying and grieving. Most dying and grieving persons call upon the minister to pray, but some will not. A chapter in *The Caregiver Journal* (1993) of College of Chaplains, Inc., "Prayer and Pastoral Care," states the following:

> The clinical training movement correctly saw that prayer was often being imposed upon sick people by the clergy and therefore regularly interfered with, rather than promoted, the pastoral care relationship. It was being used as a crutch to fill in or close a visit when the chaplain had nothing else to say. Unfortunately, rather than finding ways to integrate prayer, it was too often abandoned as a pastoral care tool.[4]

This need not be so. Personal prayer, family prayer times, and prayers in the religious communities of faith have always been valued for giving thanks, gaining support, finding strength, and increasing faith. In death and grief sustenance and reconciliation is discovered afresh. The writers of "Prayer and Pastoral Care" suggest incisively that there are those ". . . who are working to recapture prayer as an important integrated component of our pastoral care."[5] They emphasize the importance of prayer as Assessment, which means "Spiritual diagnosis . . . can happen during prayer." Prayer is also seen as "connection, a bridge." It connects the person to self, to the minister, and to God.[6] It serves to "deepen the level of intimacy between the chaplain and the patient" and helps to make ". . . a connection to God, especially to a God of forgiveness, strength and reconciliation."[7]

The questions "When," "How," and "Where," arise and call for answers. The dying and grieving provide clues if our sensitivities are attuned. These persons are better served when prayers are specific. "What would you like us to remember?" or "So that our prayer may be meaningful to you, would you like us to remember anything in particular?" help to open doors of communication and to give indications for future ministry. The absence of a request for prayer should not deter the minister from offering a prayer. On the other hand, one need not feel compelled to pray each time he visits a dying or grieving person or in every encounter.

Aside from the physical conditions in view of the patient's emotions and spirit, there are choice moments that are conducive to offering prayer. It is appropriate to have a prayer with the dying or grieving when he has shared a meaningful religious experience. The crisis of illness causes one to look into his own life in ways that produce religious experiences not encountered at any other time or under any other circumstances. When one is ill he is forced to grapple with his own humanness and likely becomes more religious than at other times. He is dealing with ultimate issues in his illness more so than in the days of good health.

Another appropriate time for prayer occurs when a person makes confession of particular sins or of his failure to live up to his own expectations or to God's expectations. Once a person has confessed, prayer is appropriate.

There are times when a prayer of thanksgiving can be offered. When the dying or grieving has dealt with his coming death and has come to an experience of inner peace and contentment, prayer is appropriate. Prayers of thanksgiving are proper when the dying patient has resolved troublesome relationships or when reconciliation with another has occurred.

It is comforting for the minister to pray with bereaved families, provided it is a prayer which does not heighten anxiety or create guilt within those survivors of the deceased. Commonly, prayer offered at critical junctures or separation communicates to the grief sufferer that he is joined in community with his fellow human sufferers, his family, his church, and his God. To be joined in community helps to ease the pain of isolation that the sufferer so deeply feels.

It is a good practice to linger for awhile after prayer has been offered with a dying patient or with the bereaved family. Prayer sometimes helps a person to express deep emotions and personal feelings. The experience of prayer can become evocative of feelings that can seldom surface in any other way.

The manner of prayer is important. The minister should aspire to pray in a conversational tone and avoid preaching. Prayer that is conversational in tone, nature, and content conveys personal concern. Prayers should be brief. Sometimes the shortest prayers are the best remembered. Doubtless prayers are more meaningful when they are to the point and concrete in nature. Long prayers tire anyone, especially the dying patient and the grieving survivor. Long prayers also are lost on both dying and grieving persons, since attention span is brief. Preoccupations are so intense that longer prayers have less value than shorter ones. Support, trust, and assurance are important in prayers for the dying and the bereaved and need to be thought out carefully.

The content of prayer should deal with concerns within the limits of reality. Primarily prayer should serve to give strength. A prayer outside the bounds of reality has the possible destructive effect of damaging the faith system of the dying patient or that of the bereaved. For a minister to pray for the recovery of a person whose medical resources have been exhausted and who cannot live causes serious consequences for a family who has a deep faith in God. Prayers for "the will of God to be done" communicate the possibility that God is uncaring and humankind powerless to do more than submit without question. Prayers of this nature do little to satisfy the human soul.

The content of prayer for bereaved persons should include the mention of the profound experiences suffered by those who are left, the need for God's help in the days of memorial arrangements, the articulation of the worthwhileness of the person who has died, the importance of God's strength in the future days of readjustment to life, and the affirmation of hope for the future. The use of familiar Scripture passages in the prayers is a source of comfort and stability for those caught up in the trauma of emotional and spiritual suffering. It reminds them of the faith by which they and their beloved have lived, and of the faith that is present even in the death experience itself.

The content of prayers should be patient-centered for the dying and person-centered for the grieving. Vague generalities, trite cliches, platitudes, and overly sentimental assurances should be avoided. A prayer that captures the feelings of the dying or the grieving, in preference to intellectualized ideas, personalizes prayer. Polite prayers that leave raw emotions untouched and unexplored are ineffective. The minister who is sensitive to the wide range of possible feelings experienced by the sufferer will be able to help him deal with these feelings in the future.

SACRAMENTS, ORDINANCES, AND RITUALS

Each religious order has its own religious philosophy of sacraments and ordinances. Regardless of the minister's own viewpoint, it is important to be aware of meaningful personal and family rituals held in value and practiced by the dying and the grieving. The minister's responsibility is to rise above theological differences and to seek forms, customs, and rituals that are meaningful to the persons themselves. Some ministers feel uncomfortable in conducting a ritual which is not a part of their own theological or religious community. If a minister feels extremely uncomfortable or awkward in carrying out a ritual it is better to call upon the minister of the patient's or family's particular religious order because of the meaning that the ritual has for the dying or bereaved. If this is impossible, then the minister must consider the significance of the ritual for those persons involved, and graciousness and respectfulness become important.

Sacramental ministries carry much value for someone who is dying. It enables him to feel a part of his community of faith. The minister is aware that sacramental ministries have profound emotional and spiritual value in helping a person to solidify the deeper commitment of his soul.

Communion and eucharist signify celebration and thanksgiving. Souls are nurtured and connected to the church's historic beliefs regarding forgiveness, grace, and hope in God's mercy through observance of the Holy Eucharist.

The minister, chaplain, priest, rabbi, and pastor become positioned to provide meaningful ministries when conversant with the rituals and practices of various denominations and religious orders. It is important for pastors and chaplains to learn from other faith structures and practices which religious resources are meaningful— Protestants learning from Catholics and Jews; Jews from Catholics and Protestants; Catholics from Jews and Protestants.

Confession has its place of importance in all three faiths. Most ministers are aware of the value of the sacrament of Holy Communion and of its meaning to the dying Roman Catholic patient. A new understanding is realized concerning the custom of anointing, formally regarded as extreme unction. Appreciation of how helpful this is to a dying patient should be sensed by each minister who works with the dying. It is helpful to remember that when a stillbirth occurs baptism is desired, and although a priest is preferred and should be called, another Christian believer, or a non-Christian can baptize the deceased as well. While most ministers are aware of the importance attached to the sacrament of baptism by Roman Catholics, they are unaware that a nonbeliever can perform this rite in extreme circumstances.

Jewish law regards the dying patient with sacredness. Making him comfortable physically and helping him settle accounts emotionally and spiritually is emphasized. Importance is attached to confession on the part of the dying Jewish patient. Not only is the rabbi important, but when he is unavailable the president of the synagogue can hear the confession of the dying person. This failing, other persons present qualify as confessors. Confession becomes exceedingly important as a means of verbalizing one's regrets as well as aspirations. Knowledge of the practice of embalming in Jewish life is important to pastors. Embalming is not generally practiced except in instances in which the deceased cannot be buried or cremated within a reasonable time. The memorial service preferably is held on the day of the death, in which case embalming becomes unnecessary. When the service cannot be done the same day, embalming is indicated and is customarily done. This sketchy presentation does not do justice to the fuller range of any faith and practice of religious beliefs and customs. Better still is the minister's need to learn more of faiths other than his own.

These are only a few of the practices considered important by faiths other than Protestant and these vary from one locale to another, and from one branch to another in major faiths and denominations. In a more cosmopolitan and pluralistic world, pastors find it necessary to acquaint themselves with religious beliefs and practices of others. This is not only for the sake of courtesy but also for the maximum help which he can be to those who are dying or grieving.

RELIGIOUS LITERATURE

The use of wisely chosen religious literature for the grieving person has value. One of the dangers of the use of literature is that it can become a substitute for an incarnational relationship between the dying and the living. For some ministers it is safer to leave a tract or a devotional booklet with a dying patient or with a grieving family than it is to offer oneself in compassion and concern. Timing and the nature of the content are crucial to the use or disuse of literature. The personality of the individual, the physical condition, and the nature of the person's spiritual disposition enter into whether or not we give any literature to the dying or to the bereaved. Use of literature has only relative value. Giving helpful reading material to either the dying or grieving at certain points in their experience can be of value. It is better perhaps to leave reading matter with the dying or with the bereaved with the understanding that whatever questions are raised could be further discussed. Great care should be given to the reading matter itself and necessitates extreme caution and careful evaluation of the contents beforehand. It is advisable to wait until the person requests devotional literature, booklets, and other written resources, thus indicating their readiness for such materials.

PREPARING THE LIVING TO DEAL WITH DEATH

Preparation for dealing with death and grief is a vital part of the pastor's ministry. Group discussions, sermons, conversations with parishioners, and parish workshops are useful media in preparation. Having participated in a grief seminar, an elderly gentleman of deep faith and personal resources said, "Having recently lost my son who was an illustrious physician, I think I experienced all of the emotional responses and reactions that were mentioned in this seminar tonight."

Ministers who use the pulpit for educating members in the nature of dying and grief will discover how meaningful preparation is in helping them to face death and its grief. As stated elsewhere, pastors may wish to include these topics in yearly sermon planning. Persons then learn to normalize feelings they have formerly abnormalized. Intellectual and emotional preparation in advance of the crisis has value in healthy emotional and spiritual adjustment.

THE COMMUNITY OF FAITH

Whenever persons are in grief, other friends and members in those persons' community of faith become uniquely meaningful to them. The faith they have shared in worship, companionship, and common crises serves to knit their hearts and souls together.

> The Christian community has intuitively provided ways and means of ministering to the grief of persons, and the pastor can depend upon the help of his congregation to help take care of the bereaved persons. . . . The pastor is the only trained person to whose hands the care of the bereaved is wholly committed at the time of the crisis. He has no competition here from other professions.[8]

The pastor's emotional maturity and pastoral posture determines in large measure the quality of support offered by the congregation. When a member of the fellowship is in grief, the community response has little to do with dogma. More often than not the intuitive and emotive bond of relationship that exists is of more importance than ecclesiastical or theological concerns. Closeness which pervades the caring community does not submit to the rigors of creedal consistency. Grieving persons simply "feel" the rhythms of concern, of closeness, of support of each other in faith. "The importance of community in one's reaffirmation is obvious."[9] At each point of the grief process the support of friends encourages him to accept his loss and not to despair of love. "A final guideline to the pastor's ministry to the bereaved, then, is a reiteration of the positive effects of a supporting community.[10] Aside from the value of and necessity for community, there are several practical results of the community's concern. Jackson (1963) suggests:

1. Community is important to the bereaved because grief and loss are more readily admitted in a group than when one is alone.
2. Community support is beneficial . . . in the affirmation of meaning.
3. Finally the life of the congregation is important as the bereaved seeks to establish new relationships and to reaffirm life. It gives him room to make "false starts." It offers him an opportunity to test his new identity. The confidence of the congregation in him and their affection for him enable him to work out the meaning of his new life. They are, in short, the patient's friends who stand with him while he learns to live and love again.[11]

Exacting as it may be and emotionally draining as it is, there is no resource which humans have to offer that is of more value to the grief sufferer than community. One who has experienced community at any previous point in his life knows how important it is in the loss of a friend or family member.

If you are actively related to the life of a religious group, you will find that it has a deeper meaning to you now than ever before, for one of its purposes is to sustain life in times of crisis. If you have not had any connection with a religious group, you may find a strength there now that you had not imagined.[12]

Hardly any satisfaction is more rewarding to the one who extends his love to the grief sufferer than that of "being community."

THE FUNERAL SERVICE

The funeral service has potential for becoming a valuable religious resource and provides the opportunity for individual and corporate grief work. Hopefully, care is taken in purpose and design of the service so that grief work is not inhibited.

> The religious rites and practices surrounding the process of mourning can help the bereaved individual to engage all his feelings in a framework that makes them not only acceptable but also easily expressible. . . . the group practices that make the person feel comfortable with his own deep feelings speed the normal work of mourning and help prevent those delayed reactions that are the product of unresolved grief feelings.[13]

The minister is the key person in preparing and conducting the Memorial Service. Irion (1988) speaks about the minister's importance thus:

> His attitude in the presence of the bereaved, his manner in conducting a service, his integrity in self-possession, having important bearing upon the therapeutic effect of the funeral . . . we must admit that one way in which something is said may make a more helpful impression on the mourners than what is said. An understanding manner is a prerequisite for a therapeutic funeral, no matter how carefully it is prepared.[14]

The American Way of Death[15] is a strong condemnation of funeral practices, of burials, and of handling death. This book points out a number of abuses of the American way of handling funerals. Though it is extremely critical of all funeral practices, it does have merit in confronting our culture with its extravagances. Granted, much of what Mitford (1963) contends needs to be evaluated. Her criticisms, though somewhat unfair in some of her generalizations, serve as important reminders that the funeral needs to be put in proper perspective. It is true that there are malpractices on the part of unscrupulous morticians. While there is good reason to believe that abuses exist with regard to evaluation of cost and to customs, there are also many concerned, reputable morticians. Their sensitivities to family needs, to emotional trauma, to the desire to make their last act of love one of sacrifice, incline them to be of much assistance. Morticians of character and integrity are aware that families sometimes attempt to pay off their debt of guilt to the deceased by extravagances. Morticians are becoming more and more aware of the emotional and psychic dynamics of grieving persons and are doing much to help to cushion the frightening and painful experiences that strike families in their loss.

The minister can be of help to the family and the morticians in keeping costs in hand, but more important is his role in helping the funeral service to be of maximum emotional and spiritual value. Jackson suggests, "A healthy ceremonial is one that provides an appropriate setting in which people can easily express legitimate feelings related to important events in their lives or in the life of the group."[16] Appropriate expression of feelings has been emphasized earlier. The funeral should be designed toward healthy expression, release, and adjustment to the experience of loss.

A funeral will serve as a healthy ceremonial when it helps the individuals in a community to accept rather than deny their feelings; moreover, it serves helpful ends when it is conducted in an atmosphere that permits facing reality not only personally but socially.[17] Although some churchmen would like very much to deny this, Irion (1954) is doubtless correct in his following observation.

> Many of the ceremonies and rites of the church have become devoid of meaning to people because of their lack of concern with human needs. If they are allowed to become rites which are performed only for the sake of themselves without

due recognition of individual needs and an effort to meet these needs, they can hardly be expected to become sufficient events in movement of the spirit of God into the lives of men.[18]

Bowen (1986), a family systems therapist, in speaking of the function of funerals, endorses my long-held views concerning the value, function, and appropriateness of the funeral ritual as an aid and necessity for wholesome grief adjustment.

The funeral ritual has existed in some form since man became a civilized being. It serves a common function of bringing survivors into intimate contact with the dead and with important friends, and it helps survivors and friends to terminate their relationship with the dead and to move forward with life. I think the best function of a funeral is served when it brings relatives and friends into the best possible functional contact with the harsh fact of death and with each other at this time of high emotionality. I believe funerals were probably more effective when people died at home with the family present, and when family and friends made the coffin and did the burial themselves.[19]

It could well be added, ". . . and dug the grave and placed the remains in the family cemetery, with the corpse having lain in state in the family's home." Bowen also believes that the entire family should be involved, even children when possible, open caskets are important, that the funeral should be personalized and that . . . the goal is to bring the entire family system into the closest possible contact with death in the presence of the total friendship system. . . .[20]

Death is a family experience. It is also a community experience. Funeral ceremonials which speak of the "democracy of death"; "no man is an island"; "none liveth to himself and none dieth to himself" help to reinforce the reality of community. Since dying and death so intimately involve all persons, family, friends, and community experiences loss, are pained, and do grieve.

The funeral must speak to human needs if it is to be meaningful to the mourner and to the community of fellow mourners. Together the funeral director and minister must confront those human needs and must seek to meet them. No one else has access to the knowledge of these needs because of morticians and ministers intense and durative experiences with grieving persons. Jackson's (1964) practical suggestions for leading mourners through these stressful circumstances are as follows:

- A funeral must face the reality of death—not avoid it.
- A funeral must provide a setting wherein the religious needs of the bereaved must be satisfied.
- A funeral must provide faith to sustain your spirit.
- A funeral must help you express your feelings.
- A funeral must help free you from guilt or self-condemnation.
- A funeral must direct you beyond the death of the loved on to the responsibilities of life.
- A funeral must, in a personal way, help you face a crisis with dignity and courage.
- A funeral must above all provide an environment where loving friends and relatives can give you the help you need to face the future with strength and courage.[21]

Chapter 6

The Pastor's Unique Function in Death's Crises

Two questions are primary in the minister's grief work. "What is the minister's uniqueness in grief ministry?" "How does the minister function effectively?" The first question is a matter of role, while the second is a matter of how he performs his art.

First, the minister is uniquely equipped by his calling, his emotional maturity, his spiritual disposition, and his pastoral training to be and to do in grief what no one else can do. The physician, the nurse, and other members of the medical team have their unique function in working with and ministering to the needs of the dying patient and the family of one who has died. Yet, no one stands at precisely the same critical place as does the minister at the time of grief. Bachman (1964) says the following:

> The image of the pastor is one that emphasizes, among other symbolizations, the spirit of Him who came to comfort and to heal broken relationships. . . . The relationship he has had with the grief sufferer determines how much help he can bring in time of grief crises.[1]

It must be recognized that the uniqueness of his opportunity and function does not guarantee that he will be entirely adequate to the situation on every occasion. No minister ever feels completely comfortable or fully adequate in the face of grief of another. To recognize his own humanity and to be conversant with the feelings which he himself experiences at the time of grief and those caused by his working with grieving persons is of importance. A part of his own burden is to deal with his own feelings and to face the reality of these feelings honestly. The teaching and training of ministers leads one to conclude that they themselves experience the same kinds of feelings that other humans do, and that the ecclesiastical collar or the certificate of ordination does not make them immune to either the tender or the tough human emotions experienced by all persons. Clothed in humanity, his life is as vulnerable to pain, anger, disappointment, guilt, love, biological drives, depressive feelings, or any other emotions or emotional state experienced by others. The minister who has difficulty in acknowledging and coming to terms with his feelings is advised to seek the kind of professional help, either counseling, psychiatric, or other by which he can come to recognize and to deal with his own feelings. Sensitivity is of paramount importance on the part of the pastor. He must know something of the nature and strength of his own feelings before he is in a position to help others. He must face death in himself realistically with the knowledge of his own strengths and weaknesses, the limitations of his own resources, and the knowledge of what are his own anxieties and fears. Unless he is aware and can manage these, he is likely to project feelings of his own into his relationship with the grief sufferer.

Bachman points out some basic considerations that can be summarized as a need to have a genuine love for patients for themselves, a need for practice in his skills, a sensitivity to others, an awareness of both his and the grief sufferer's limitations, and a need to be a good listener.[2] Still others are critical. To start with the person where he is, to accept a person where he is irrespective of agreement with the premises or the presuppositions of the grieving person, to seek to clarify feelings, to indicate choices and alternatives, and to be cautious in making interpretations are all necessary ingredients to successful grief work.

As the minister practices his art it is necessary to encourage talking, crying, and emoting with the grieving person. Seeking to be of comfort at times of death, friends or relatives may say to the grief sufferer, "Don't cry. Be brave. God will give you strength." Is it a sin to cry? Not if one remembers John's gospel account (John 11:35) which says, "Jesus wept." Jesus did weep because of the hurt that came when his friend Lazarus died. Our theologies and beliefs do not serve us well if it is understood as forbidding us to cry when in pain or that showing emotion is a sign of weakness. To cry is to respond to a God-given emotion and is among the safest and most therapeutic of all emotional safety valves. Genuine cleansing can occur. Ethnic groups who feel permission to emote freely, and can do this when grieving, experience its helpfulness. Expression of intense emotion makes for better, more wholesome emotional adjustment to loss. Those who feel that crying is a weakness find more difficulty in adjusting to deep loss.

It is also a valuable experience to talk about the deceased. Frequently family members and pastors cause the grieving person to suppress genuine feelings by changing the subject of conversation despite the need for the grieving person to talk about the deceased. This is a disservice. The grieving person needs permission to talk about the one who has died. The helpfulness of verbalizing feelings in grief work is undeniable. Despite the importance of talking, and crying, permission to remain silent and withdrawn is important to those who have difficulty showing emotion.

The pastor can give help to the grieving person by accepting and hearing whatever feelings are emerging. It takes time and experience to learn to be a creative listener. Previous education and training, along with anxiety which comes with crises, cause some ministers to have difficulty in refraining from talking. Unwittingly ministers may dominate the conversation and by talking take away the opportunity of the bereaved to grieve. Some grievers may express feelings of hostility and hatred, even toward God, or they may express warm and tender feelings. Care should be taken to allow persons to express hostility toward God for feelings of unfairness at the death of the valued and loved person. It is not necessary for the minister to defend God; this communicates to the grieving person that it is shameful to attack God. The minister should remember the impiety and audacity of Jeremiah who boldly remonstrated with God, or Jesus who confessed to feelings of forsakenness by God. God does not need the pastor's defense—the grief sufferer does not need the pastor's judgment.

The pastor helps by giving emotional and spiritual support; at times the grieving person is comforted by physical touch. There is meaningful ministry in appropriate and discreet physical touch. One who is hurting feels better at the physical touch of someone else. Physical touch is difficult for some, but if the minister encounters a grieving person at a funeral home looking at the body of the deceased and does not give the physical support of touch to the griever, he may be perceived as insensitive and uncaring. Despite how others may interpret physical touch, this is often meaningful and healing. The experience is important to many persons who have felt a communication of humanness and divineness when the minister has embraced them at the time of their deep need. Emotional and spiritual support is given in this way. The value of the ministry of touch cannot be underestimated. It becomes a link with the real world of persons, and is a potent nonverbal form of communication of human emotions between persons. Emotional and spiritual support are communicated by touch but must not be done to excess.

The minister can also render emotional and spiritual support through being a human who understands the deep hurt that grievers are experiencing. Dr. Richard Young, who has taught so many things to so many ministers, emphasized over and over again that the presence of a minister is of utmost importance at the time of grief. He contended that it is far better "to be the love of God than to talk about it." There is no human experience of suffering that cannot be made more bearable by the minister's being the Love of God.

The minister is meaningful to the grieving person as he offers the support of his own religious faith. Reassurance is given in the sharing of faith through which the grieving person is enabled to actualize his own spiritual faith and resources. The minister by his calling is expected to give reassurance with the gospel, if he be a Christian minister; or he will be expected to offer the resources of the church, the synagogue or temple, or whatever other religious body he represents. He will be looked to by the grief sufferer as one who possesses qualities, skill, knowledge, and insight, growing out of his own training and serious wrestling with ultimate concerns. The leader of the religious order to which the grieving or dying belongs has the responsibility of helping the person to find meaningfulness in suffering and death wherever he is in his religious pilgrimage. Through creatively cultivated relationships with family members of the deceased, the minister becomes a person of critical importance to grief sufferers. They look to him for some word from God that will bring solace and comfort at the time of their loss. In this way he becomes God's love.

The minister is a friend to the dying and grieving. The effective minister chooses to incarnate a spirit of caring. Through relationships he has been found to be sensitive to hurt and compassionate in spirit. Through relationships he befriends. It is questionable how much the minister can constructively help grief sufferer without the existence of a deep bond of friendship between the minister and the griever. The quality of friendship that is vital in death's crisis is one characterized by compassion, sincerity, authenticity, and transparency.

It is important to grieving persons to have a minister who can serve as a trustworthy confessor. A grieving person often experiences guilt that may or may not be reality based. Every minister at one time or another is seen as a mediator for confession of sin to God. This becomes especially true in grief work. A grieving person will find himself caught up by conflict, anxiety, guilt, and ambivalence regarding the deceased. Relationships between persons exist in curious forms, so when deep loss is sustained the conscious mind brings back a wide range of experiences in which the survivor experiences guilt, remorse, and regret. The minister has a responsibility to take seriously whatever feelings of guilt are expressed by a grieving person. In *The Dynamics of Confession* (1969)[3] I suggest how confessional ministry can be practiced, and notes that the confessor has a profound responsibility to lead the guilt-ridden person to realize the assurance of forgiveness. It is important that he take seriously whatever feelings of guilt are expressed by one who is confessing. While much guilt associated with grief is unrealistic in nature, there are obviously a number of incidents in the grieving person's life in which he experienced true guilt over relationships with the deceased. These feelings need to be taken seriously and need to be dealt with in such a way that the bereaved person can acknowledge the feelings and experience the assurance of God's forgiveness.

The minister becomes a clarifier of reality and truth. The objectivity that comes from seeing the bereaved person's and family's situation in perspective, both temporary and ultimate, implies that he is both responsible for giving honest reflection of reality and for helping a person to face acknowledged realities. Sometimes he is able to perform a very vital service by simply standing outside the situation and bringing a person and family to face the real world rather than becoming bogged down in emotional recrimination and self-blame.

This is done by helping to objectify reality with respect to medical treatment given to the deceased, with respect to funeral arrangements, or with respect to enabling the bereaved to make satisfying and fulfilling adjustment to his loss.

By the nature of his calling, the minister becomes a cocreator of renewal and redemption. He functions in the grief situation in much the same way as he does in all his pulpit and pastoral ministries. He is involved in partnership with God. The whole process of bringing to bear the resources that lead to reconstruction of life, to renewal, and to reclamation are integral to his ministry. The witness of his lifestyle and his faith system issues in incarnate proclamation of good news in the midst of bad news. He becomes the Isaiah who proclaims, "Comfort ye, comfort ye, my people." He is responsible for bringing to bear creative energies and resources of the God who cares for those who are undone and devastated by the trauma of loss, of separation, and of death. The minister presents himself to those in need by the offering of himself in incarnated relationships of love, understanding, acceptance, and concern.

The minister serves as educator to his congregation. Through this pulpit ministry and his teaching, he has opportunity to help his flock become aware of emotions which are normally experienced in dying and death. It is a good practice perhaps to preach sermons periodically on some of the expected responses experienced in grief (some ministers feel once each year is desirable). This helps to acquaint the congregation with some of the emotions that are part of dying and of the grief process. Practical ways and steps by which persons and families can prepare to face death in themselves or a loved one can be provided by sermons, discussions, and classes. As church members later experience dying and death, assistance in claiming the normalcy of the dying and grieving shall have been provided, as well as clearer insights into personal grief and family grief.

Westberg's work[4] is well worth recommending to those who are experiencing grief because of the help it provides in understanding normal reactions and responses to grief. Persons and families feel less abnormal, less strange, when it is recognized that others have similar experiences when crisis strikes. Dying persons and grief sufferers are likely to experience distortion of normal feelings and to feel guilty for having had these feelings or feeling states. Among these are fear, depression, anger, confusion, guilt, and loneliness. When the minister reassures congregants of the normality of these feelings, it both aids persons in expressing these and helps persons to be more honest with themselves and others in grief.

The minister is the recognized religious educator. As he functions pastorally, as he preaches, as he instructs, and as he lives before his people, he is perpetually involved in religious education. He is looked to for helpful instruction about the meaning of life.

> Religious teaching recognizes the mystery of life. The elements of true mysteries become more mysterious than all we know of them. So, with life, the more we know the more we are aware of the fact that we know little or nothing about the origin or final end of life except as it is made known to us through our religious faith. In time of crisis this faith becomes unusually important.
>
> Death is a great mystery. . . . What we feel about death tends to show what we feel about life. If death is a blotting out of all there was of an individual, then the value of life itself is decreased. But if death is like another birth, there are new possibilities for an emerging life . . . .[5]

Religious teaching before, during, and after the crisis of death helps one to become related to reality, to wholesomeness of grief recovery, and to spiritual hope in the midst of humanness and death.

> Religion helps a person to look up and out and not down and out. It helps him to give expression to a living faith that is not measured by physical life alone. It ties him to eternal things when he needs them most. It is not without reason that the community entrusts the care of the bereaved to the religious leaders of its group life. Their experience with life and death, their understanding of people, and their own faith, makes them valuable to us when we seek to emerge from the depths of our grief.[6]

There is no other sure comfort to religious persons than one's religious faith. There is no stronger source of solace than one's religious faith and practice. There is no more durable companion or ally in adjustment to dying and grieving than one's faith assurances.

Notes

Chapter 1

1. James W. Fowler, *Becoming Adult, Becoming Christian* (San Francisco: Harper and Row Publishers, 1984); James W. Fowler, "Sketch of Stages and Dominant Faith Development," copyrighted by Center for Faith Development; mimeographed handout to Association for Clinical Pastoral Education, Fall Conference, 1986, Atlanta, Georgia, as part of lecture presentation [Credit is given to Robert Kegan for subscriptions on ego stages, *The Evolving Self* (Cambridge, MA: Harvard University Press, 1982), pp. 118-120]; Lawrence Kohlberg, "Moral Stages and Moralization, The Cognitive-Developmental Approach," from *Moral Development and Behavior*, Thomas Lickona, Ed. (New York: Holt, Rinehart and Winston, 1976).

2. Mary Field Belenky, Blythe McVicker Clinchy, Nancy Rule Goldberger, and Jill Mattuck Tarule, *Women's Ways of Knowing* (New York: Basic Books, Inc., 1986); Carol Gilligan, *In a Different Voice* (Cambridge, MA and London, England: Harvard University Press, 1982).

3. Peter D. Lifton, "Personological and Psychodynamic Explanations," *Handbook of Moral Development*, Gary L. Sapp, Ed. (Birmingham, Alabama: Religious Education Press, 1986), p. 64.

4. *Ibid.*, pp. 66 ff., paraphrased and summarized; Lawrence Walker, "Cognitive Processes in Moral Development," Sapp, pp. 126-127.

5. Kohlberg, *op. cit.*, p. 31 ff; Charlene J. Langdale, "A ReVision of Structural-Developmental Theory," In *Handbook of Moral Development*, Sapp, Ed., (Birmingham, AL: Religious Education Press, 1986), pp. 18 ff.

6. Lawrence Kohlberg, p. 32.

7. *Ibid.*, p. 32.

8. Belenky et al; Gilligan, *op. cit.*

9. Kohlberg, pp. 34 ff.

10. James W. Fowler; the summarization and condensation attempts to be an accurate accounting of Fowler's conceptualization of faith development.

11. As noted before, Fowler credits Kegan with the subscriptive designations of "The Incorporative Self, the Impulsive Self, etc.," in Kegan's work to which reference is previously made.

12. James W. Fowler, p. 56.

13. *Ibid.*, p. 58.

14. *Ibid.*, p. 60.

15. *Ibid.*, pp. 64, 65.

16. *Ibid.*, pp. 64, 65.

17. *Ibid.*, p. 67.

18. *Ibid.*, pp. 67, 68.

19. *Ibid.*, p. 75.

20. *Ibid.*, p. 75.

21. *Ibid.*, p. 19.

22. *Ibid.*, pp. 25, 26.

23. *Ibid.*, p. 25.

24. Craig Dykstra, "What Is Faith?" *Faith Development and Fowler*, Craig Dykstra and Sharon Parks (Birmingham, AL: Religious Education Press, 1986), p. 49.

25. *Ibid.*, pp. 49 ff.

26. *Ibid.*, p. 55.

27. Langdale, p. 43.

28. Gilligan, "Introduction," p. 1.

29. *Ibid.*, p. 160.

30. *Ibid.*, p. 160.

31. *Ibid.*, p. 172.

32. Langdale, p. 17.

33. Belenky, "Introduction," pp. 6, 7 ff.

34. Stated in summary fashion here from a presentation by a colleague, Mary Catherine Hasty, in an unpublished presentation to the Supervisory Staff Conference at North Carolina Baptist Hospitals, Inc., School of Pastoral Care, Fall 1987.

35. *Ibid.*

36. Belenky et al., p. 229.

37. Alfred B. Pasteur and Ivory L. Toldson, *Roots of Soul* (New York, Garden City: Anchor Press/Doubleday, 1982), p. 4.

38. *Ibid.*, pp. 4, 5.

39. *Ibid.*, p. 7.

40. *Ibid.*, p. 9.

41. *Ibid.*, pp. 17, 18, quoting Lilyan Kesteloot, *Black Writers in French*, translated by Ellen Conroy Kennedy (Philadelphia: Temple University Press, 1984, p. 106).

42. *Ibid.*, p. 8.

43. *Ibid.*, pp. 18, 19.

44. *Ibid.*, paraphrase summary, pp. 78, 79.

45. *Ibid.*, p. 80.

46. *Ibid.*, p. 112.

Chapter 2

1. John W. James and Frank Cherry, *The Grief Recovery Handbook* (New York: Harper & Row, 1989), p. 43.

2. Barbara M. Newman and Philip R. Newman, *Development Through Life: A Psychological Approach* (Pacific Grove, CA.: Brooks/Cole Publishing Company, 1991), p. 40.

3. *Ibid.*, p. 43.

4. *Ibid.*

5. James Maurice Briggs, "Presentation of Family Systems," Clinical Pastoral Education Supervisory Theory Seminar, Department of Clinical Pastoral Education of North Carolina Baptist Medical Center, Winston-Salem, NC, February 24, 1988, (Summarization).

6. Karl Augustus Menninger, Martin Mayman, and Paul Pruyser, *The Vital Balance* (New York: The Viking Press, 1963), pp. 76, 77, 78.

7. Briggs.

8. Briggs.

9. Newman and Newman, p. 47.

10. Newman and Newman, p. 47.

11. W.R. Beavers, *Psychotherapy and Growth: A Family Systems Perspective* (New York: Brunner/Mazel, 1976); Murray Bowen, *Family Therapy in Clinical Practice* (Northvale, NJ and London: Jason Aronson, 1986, New Printing); Jerry M. Lewis, *To Be a Therapist* (New York: Brunner/Mazel, Publishers, 1978, second printing); Edwin H. Friedman, *From Generation to Generation* (New York and London: Guilford Press, 1985); Augustus Y. Napier and Carl A. Whittaker, *The Family Crucible—One Family's Therapy—An Experience That Illuminates All Our Lives* (New York: Bantam Books, 1980).

12. Edwin H. Friedman, *From Generation to Generation* (New York and London: Guilford Press, 1985), p. 23.

13. Augustus Y. Napier and Carl A. Whittaker, *The Family Crucible* (New York: Bantam Books, 1980), pp. 86, 87.

14. Friedman, p. 34.

15. Murray Bowen, *Family Therapy in Clinical Practice* (Northvale, NJ and London: 1986, new printing), an author's paraphrase and summarizations from Bowen; restated, pp. 170 ff.

16. Bowen, p. 199.

17. Bowen, p. 328.

18. Bowen, p. 86.

19. Bowen, p. 325.

20. Bowen.

21. Bowen, p. 327.

22. Friedman, pp. 162-190.

23. Paraphrase, summarization of Friedman, pp. 162-190.

Chapter 3

1. Liston O. Mills, Ed., *Perspectives on Death* (Nashville and New York: Abingdon Press, 1969), p. 253.

2. *Ibid.*, p. 254.

3. Paul H. Braner, MD, Eleanor Cockesill. Bernard Kutscher, PhD, and others, *A Constructive Approach to Terminal Illness* (New York: National Cancer Foundation, Inc., N.D.), summary of ideas.

4. Jocelyn Evans, *Living with a Man Who Is Dying* (New York: Tamlinger Publishing Company, 1971), flyleaf.

5. *Ibid.*, p. 133.

6. Mills, p. 262.

7. Herman Feifel, Ed., *The Meaning of Death* (New York, London, Sydney, Toronto: McGraw-Hill Book Company, Inc., 1959), p. 123.

8. David Hendin, *Death as a Fact of Life* (New York: W. W. Norton and Company, Inc., 1973), p. 99, quoting Herman Feifel.

9. Paul Tillich, "The Theology of Pastoral Care," *Pastoral Psychology*, X, October, 1959, pp. 226, 227.

10. Kenneth R. Mitchell, *Hospital Chaplain* (Philadelphia: The Westminster Press, 1972), pp. 88-91.

11. Heije Faber, *Pastoral Care in the Modern Hospital* (Philadelphia: The Westminster Press, copyright by SCM Press, 1971), p. 66.

12. Mills, p. 254.

13. Hendin, p. 99.

14. Mitchell, pp. 88-91.

15. *Ibid.*, p. 88 f.

16. Feifel, p. 126.

17. *Ibid.*, p. 128.

18. Sherwin B. Nuland, *How We Die* (New York: Alfred A. Knopf, 1994), p. 20.

19. *Ibid.*, pp. 20, 21.

20. Sandol Stoddard, *The Hospice Movement* (Briarcliff Manor, New York: Stein and Day Publishers, 1978), pp. 63, 64.

21. National Hospice Organization brochure, "Hospice in America 1979" and updated almost annually.

22. Hospice of Winston-Salem/Forsyth County, Inc., brochure, "Serving the Terminally Ill and Their Families," 1979.

23. Kübler-Ross. I have borrowed heavily from her insights and have briefly summarized her conclusions.

24. Victor E. Frankl, *Man's Search for Meaning* (Boston: Beacon Press, 1959, 1963); *The Doctor and the Soul* (New York: Alfred A. Knopf, 1957).

25. Hendin, p. 105.

26. *Ibid.*

27. Wayne E. Oates, *The Christian Pastor* (Philadelphia: The Westminster Press, 1964, revised and enlarged edition), pp. 41 ff.

28. George W. Bowman, III, *The Dynamics of Confession* (Richmond: John Knox Press, 1965), pp. 55-60.

29. Glenn Mosby, "Acceptance," *Death and Bereavement*, edited by Austin H. Kutscher (Springfield, IL: Charles C Thomas, 1969), p. 234.

30. Steven B. Mizel and Peter Jaret, *The Human Immune System: The New Frontier in Medicine* (New York: Simon and Schuster, Inc., 1985), p. 11.

31. *Ibid.*, p. 35.

32. *Ibid.*, pp. 35, 36.

33. John Langone, *AIDS: The Facts* (Boston and Toronto: Little, Brown and Company, 1988), pp. 200-210.

34. Elisabeth Kübler-Ross, *AIDS: The Ultimate Challenge* (New York: Macmillan Publishing Company and London: Collier Macmillan Publishers, 1987).

35. Cynthia T. Morse, OEF, "Suffering and the Love of God: A Theology for Pastoral Care of People Living and Dying With HIV/AIDS," (*The Caregiver Journal*, 10(4), 1993, College of Chaplains, Inc., Schaumberg, IL), p. 20.

36. *Ibid.*

37. *Ibid.*, p. 21.

38. *Ibid.*, p. 22.

39. Langone, addendum at end of work.

Chapter 4

1. Edgar Jackson, *For the Living* (Des Moines, Iowa: Channel Press, 1963), p. 22.

2. *Ibid.*, p. 23,

3. Hardy Clemons, *Saying Goodbye to Your Grief* (Macon, GA: Smyth & Helwys Publishing Company, Inc., 1994), pp. 4-14.

4. *Ibid.*, pp. 5-21.

5. Erich Lindeman, "Symptomatology and Management of Acute Grief," *The American Journal of Psychiatry*, September 1944, pp. 163-164.

6. Granger Westberg, *Good Grief* (Philadelphia: Fortress Press, 1962), pp. 13-49.

7. Paul Irion, *The Funeral and The Mourners* (New York and Nashville: Abingdon Press, 1954), pp. 60-61.

8. Jackson, *For the Living*, pp. 18, 19.

9. Cort R. Flynt, *Grief's Slow Wisdom* (Anderson, SC: Drake House, 1976, Second Printing), p. 18.

10. Jackson, *For the Living*, p. 25.

11. Paul Tillich, *The Courage to Be* (New Haven: Yale University Press, 1952), p. 43.

12. Regina Flesch, "The Condolence Call," *Death and Bereavement*, Austin Kutscher, Ed. (Springfield, IL: Charles C Thomas, Publisher, 1969), p. 245.

13. *Ibid.*, p. 246.

14. Sherwin B. Nuland, *How We Die* (New York: Alfred A. Knopf, 1994), p. 13.

15. *Ibid.*, p. 7.

16. C. Charles Bachman, *Ministering to the Grief Sufferer* (Englewood Cliffs, NJ: Prentice Hall, 1964), p. 14.

17. Edgar N. Jackson, *You and Your Grief* (New York: Channel Press, 1961; Fifteenth Printing, 1964), p. 27.

18. Edgar N. Jackson, "Attitudes in Our Culture," *Death and Bereavement*, edited by Austin H. Kutscher (Springfield, IL: Charles C Thomas, Publisher, 1969, pp. 217, 218.

19. *Ibid.*, p. 218.

20. John W. James and Frank Cherry, *The Great Recovery Handbook* (New York: Harper & Row, 1989), p. 35.

21. Robert Fulghum, *From Beginning to End* (New York: Villard Books, 1995).

22. *Ibid.*, Frontispiece.

23. Austin H. Kutscher, "Practical Aspects of Bereavement," *Loss and Grief: Its Psychological Management in Medical Practice*, Bernard Schoenberg and others, Eds. (New York and London: Columbia University Press, 1970; Second Edition, 1971), p. 283.

24. Austin H. Kutscher, "Time," *Death and Bereavement*, edited by Austin H. Kutscher (Springfield, IL: Charles C Thomas, Publisher, 1969), pp. 309-310.

25. Edgar Jackson, *For the Living*, p. 35.

26. Kutscher, p. 310.

27. Kutscher, "Renewal," pp. 313-316.

28. Edgar Jackson, "Grief and Religion," *The Meaning of Death*, Herman Feifel, Ed. (New York: McGraw-Hill Book Company, 1965), p. 225.

29. *Ibid.*, p. 220.

30. Clemons, pp. 31-38.

Chapter 5

1. Edgar Jackson, *You and Your Grief* (New York: Channel Press, Fifth Printing, 1964), p. 55.

2. Heije Faber, *Pastoral Care in the Modern Hospital* (Philadelphia: The Westminster Press, copyright by SCM Press, 1971), p. 51.

3. Edgar Jackson, "Grief and Religion," *The Meaning of Death*, edited by Herman Feifel (New York, London, Sydney, and Toronto: McGraw-Hill Book Company, 1959), p. 219.

4. Bruce Evanson, Sr. Elaine Goodell, P.B.V.M., George Handzo and Rabbi Stephen Shulman, "Prayer and Pastoral Care," (*The Caregiver Journal*, 10(3), 1993, College of Chaplains, Inc., Schaumberg, IL), p. 40.

5. *Ibid.*, p. 40.

6. *Ibid.*, pp. 41, 43.

7. *Ibid.*, p. 44.

8. Wayne Oates, *The Christian Pastor* (Philadelphia: Westminster Press, 1964, revised and enlarged), p. 36.

9. Liston Mills, *Perspectives on Death* (New York and Nashville: Abingdon Press, 1969), p. 281.

10. *Ibid.*

11. Mills, quoting from Edgar Jackson, *You and Your Grief* (New York: Channel Press, 1963, p. 64), p. 282.

12. Jackson, *You and Your Grief*, p. 59.

13. Jackson, "Grief and Religion," p. 229 (Paperback).

14. Paul Irion, *The Funeral and the Mourners* (New York and Nashville: Abingdon Press, 1964), pp. 171, 172.

15. Jessica Mitford, *The American Way of Death* (New York: Simon and Schuster, 1963).

16. Edgar Jackson, *For the Living*, p. 22.

17. *Ibid.*

18. Paul Irion, p. 171.

19. Murray Bowen, *Family Therapy in Clinical Practice* (Northvale, NJ and London: Jason Aronson, 1986, new printing), p. 331.

20. *Ibid.*, p. 232.

21. Edgar Jackson, *You and Your Grief*, pp. 43, 44.

Chapter 6

1. Charles C. Bachman, *Ministering to the Grief Sufferer* (Englewood Cliffs, NJ: Prentice Hall, 1964), p. 25.

2. *Ibid.*, pp. 36-37.

3. George W. Bowman, *The Dynamics of Confession* (Richmond, VA: John Knox Press, 1969), pp. 94, 95.

4. Granger, Westberg, *Good Grief* (Philadelphia: Fortress Press, 1964), pp. 21-56.

5. Edgar N. Jackson, *You and Your Grief*, (New York: Channel Press, 1961), p. 58.

6. *Ibid.*, p. 59.

Bibliography

Books

Bachman, C. Charles. *Ministering to the Grief Sufferer.* Englewood Cliffs, NJ: Prentice-Hall, Inc., 1964. The Successful Counseling Series.

Beavers, W. R. *Psychotherapy and Growth: A Family Systems Perspective.* New York: Brunner/Mazel, 1976.

Belenky, Mary Field; Clinchy, McVicker Blythe; Goldberger, Nancy Rule; and Tarule, Jill Mattuck. *Women's Ways of Knowing.* New York: Basic Books, Inc., 1986.

Bowen, Murray. *Family Therapy in Clinical Practice.* Northvale, NJ and London: Jason Aronson, 1986, New Printing.

Bowman, George W. III. *The Dynamics of Confession.* Richmond, VA: John Knox Press, 1969.

Braner, Paul H., MD; Cokesill, Eleanor; and Kutner, Bernard, PhD. *A Constructive Approach to Terminal Illness.* New York: National Cancer Foundation, Inc., no date.

Clemons, Hardy. *Saying Goodbye to Your Grief.* Macon, GA: Smyth & Helwys Publishing, Inc., 1994.

Evans, Jocelyn. *Living with a Man Who Is Dying.* New York: Tamlinger Publishing Company, 1971.

Evanson, Bruce Sr.; Elaine Goodell, P.B.V.M.; George F. Handzo; and Rabbi Stephen Shulman. "Prayer and Pastoral Care." *The Caregiver Journal,* 10(3), 1993.

Faber, Heije. *Pastoral Care in the Modern Hospital.* Philadelphia, PA: The Westminster Press, 1971.

Feifel, Herman, Ed. *The Meaning of Death.* New York, London, Sydney, and Toronto: McGraw-Hill Book Company, Inc., 1959.

Flesch, Regina. "The Condolence Call." In *Death and Bereavement,* p. 245, Austin H. Kutscher, Ed. Springfield, IL: Charles C Thomas, Publisher, 1969.

Flynt, Cort R. *Grief's Slow Wisdom.* Anderson, SC: Drake House, 1967.

Fowler, James W. "Sketch of Stages and Dominant Faith Development." Mimeographed handout as part of paper presentation to Association for Clinical Pastoral Education, Fall Conference, Atlanta, Georgia, 1986. Fowler gives credit on ego stages to Kegan, Robert, *The Evolving Self.* Cambridge, MA: The Harvard University Press, 1982.

Fowler, James W. *Becoming Adult, Becoming Christian.* San Francsico, CA: Harper and Row, Publishers, 1984.

Frankl, Victor E. *The Doctor and the Soul.* New York: Alfred A Knopf, 1957. Translated by Clara and Richard Winston.

Frankl, Victor E. *Man's Search for Meaning.* Boston, MA: Beacon Press, 1959, 1963.

Friedman, Edwin H. *From Generation to Generation.* New York and London: Guilford Press, 1985.

Fulghum, Robert. *From Beginning to End: The Rituals of our Lives.* New York: Villard Books, 1995.

Gilligan, Carol. *In a Different Voice.* Cambridge, MA and London, England: Harvard University Press, 1982.

Hendin, David. *Death as a Fact of Life.* New York: W. W. Norton and Company, 1973.

Herter, Frederic P. "The Right to Die in Dignity." In *Death and Bereavement,* pp. 15, 16. Edited by Austin H. Kutscher. Springfield, IL: Charles C Thomas, Publishers, 1969.

Irion, Paul E. *The Funeral and the Mourners.* New York and Nashville, TN: Abingdon Press, 1954.

Jackson, Edgar N. *For the Living.* Des Moines, IA: Channel Press, 1963.

Jackson, Edgar N. *You and Your Grief.* New York: Channel Press, 1961; Fifteenth Printing, 1964.

Jackson, Edgar N. "Grief and Religion." In *The Meaning of Death,* p. 225. Herman Feifel, Ed. New York, London, Sydney, and Toronto: McGraw-Hill Book Company, 1965.

Jackson, Edgar N. "Attitudes Toward Death in Our Culture." In *Death and Bereavement,* pp. 217, 218, Austin H. Kutscher, Ed. Springfield, IL: Charles C Thomas, Publishers, 1969.

James, John W., and Cherry, Frank. *The Grief Recovery Handbook.* New York: Harper & Row, Publishers, 1989.

Kasper, A. N. "The Doctor and Death." In *The Meaning of Death,* p. 269, Herman Feifel, Ed. New York: McGraw-Hall Book Company, 1959.

Kastenbaum, Robert. "Death and Bereavement in Later Life." In *Loss and Grief: Its Psychological Management in Medical Practice,* p. 51, Bernard Schoenberg, Ed. New York and London: Columbia University Press, 1971.

Kesteloot, Lilyan. *Black Writers in French.* Translated by Ellen Conroy Kennedy, pp. 17, 18. Philadelphia, PA: Temple University Press, 1984. In *Roots of Soul,* Alfred B. Pasteur and Ivory L. Toldson. Garden City, NY: Anchor Press/Doubleday, 1982.

Kohlberg, Lawrence. "Moral Stages and Moralization: The Cognitive-Developmental Approach." In *Moral Development and Behavior,* pp. 31-53. New York: Holt, Rinehart and Winston, 1976.

Kübler-Ross, Elisabeth. *AIDS: The Ultimate Challenge.* New York: Macmillan Pubishing Company; London: Collier Macmillan Company, 1987.

Kübler-Ross, Elisabeth. *On Death and Dying.* New York: The Macmillan Company, 1969.

Kutscher, Austin H., Ed. *Death and Bereavement.* Springfield, IL: Charles C Thomas, Publisher, 1969.

Kutscher, Austin H. "Renewal." In *Death and Bereavement*, pp. 313-316. Austin H. Kutscher, Ed. Springfield, IL: Charles C Thomas, Publisher, 1969.

Kutscher, Austin H. "Practical Aspects of Grief." In *Loss and Grief: Its Psychological Management in Medical Practice*, p. 283, Bernard Schoenberg, Ed. New York and London: Columbia University Press, 1970; 2d Edition, cd, 1971.

Langdale, Charlene. "A Re-Vision of Structural-Developmental Theory." In *Handbook of Moral Development*, p. 43, Gary L. Sapp, Ed. Birmingham, AL: Religious Education Press, 1986.

Langone, John. *AIDS: The Facts*. Boston and Toronto: Little, Brown and Company, 1988.

Lewis, Jerry M. *To Be a Therapist*. New York: Brunner/Mazel, Publishers, 1978; 2d Printing.

Lifton, Peter D. "Personological and Psychodynamic Explanations." In *Handbook of Moral Development*, p. 64, Gary L. Sapp, Ed. Birmingham, AL: Religious Education Press, 1986.

Marcuse, Herbert. "The Theology of Death." In *The Meaning of Death*, p. 74, Herman Feifel, Ed. New York: McGraw-Hill Book Company, 1965.

Menninger, Karl Augustus, Mayman, Martin, and Pruyser, Paul. *The Vital Balance*. New York: The Viking Press, 1963.

Mills, Liston O., ed. *Perspectives on Death*. New York and Nashville, TN: Abingdon Press, 1969.

Mitchell, Kenneth R. *Hospital Chaplain*. Philadelphia, PA: The Westminster Press, 1972.

Mitford, Jessica. *The American Way of Death*. New York: Simon and Schuster, 1963.

Mizel, Steven B., and Jaret, Peter. *The Human Immune System: The New Frontier in Medicine*. New York: Simon and Schuster, Inc., 1985.

Morse, Cynthia T., OEF. "Suffering and the Love of God: A Theology for the Pastoral Care of People Living and Dying with HIV/AIDS." *The Caregiver Journal*. 10(4), 1993.

Mosby, Glen. "Acceptance." In *Death and Bereavement*, p. 234, Austin H. Kutscher, Ed. Springfield, IL: Charles C Thomas, Publisher, 1969.

Napier, Augustus Y., and Whittaker, Carl A. *The Family Crucible–One Family's Therapy–An Experience that Illuminates All Our Lives*. New York: Bantam Books, 1980.

Newman, Barbara M., and Newman, Philip R. *Development Through Life: A Psychosocial Approach*. Brooks/Cole Publishing Company: Pacific Grove, CA, 1991.

Nuland, Sherwin B. *How We Die*. New York: Alfred A. Knopf, 1994.

Oates, Wayne E. *The Christian Pastor*. Philadelphia, PA: The Westminster Press, 1964; Revised and Enlarged.

Pasteur, Alfred B., and Toldson, Ivory L. *Roots of Soul*. New York and Garden City: Anchor Press/Doubleday, 1982.

Reeves, Robert B. Jr. "To Tell or Not to Tell the Patient." In *Death and Bereavement*, pp. 8, 9, Austin H. Kutscher, Ed. Springfield, IL: Charles C Thomas, Pubisher, 1969.

Sapp, Gary L. *Handbook of Moral Development*. Birmingham, AL: Religious Education Press, 1986.

Schoenberg, Bernard, Ed. *Loss and Grief: Its Psychological Management in Clinical Practice*. New York and London: Columbia University Press, 1971.

Stoddard, Sandol. *The Hospice Movement*. Briarcliff Manor, NY: Stien and Day Publishers, 1978.

Tillich, Paul. *The Courage to Be*. New Haven: Yale University Press, 1952, p. 43.

Wahl, C. W. "The Fear of Death." In *The Meaning of Death*, p. 17, Herman Feifel, Ed. New York: McGraw-Hill Book Company, 1969.

Walker, Lawrence. "Cognitive Processes in Moral Develompent." In *Handbook of Moral Development*, pp. 126, 127, Gary L. Sapp, Ed. Birmingham, AL: Religious Education Press, 1986.

Westberg, Granger. *Good Grief*. Philadelphia, PA: Fortress Press, 1962.

Wise, Carrol A. *The Meaning of Pastoral Care*. New York: Harper and Row, 1966.

Woodyard, David O. *To Be Human Now*. Philadelphia, PA: The Westminster Press, 1969.

Journals

Barton, David. "The Need for Including Instruction on Death and Dying in the Medical Curriculum." *The Journal of Medical Education*, 47 (March 1972): 174.

Lindemann, Erich. "Symptomatology and Management of Acute Grief." *The American Journal of Psychiatry*, (September 1944): 163-164.

Tillich, Paul. "The Theology of Pastoral Care." *Pastoral Psychology*, X (October 1959): 225-236.

Pamphlets

Chelsea Psychotherapy Associates of Manhattan. Brochure offering advice on how to deal with AIDS victims. 1988.

Hospice of Winston-Salem/Forsyth County, Inc. Brochure. *Serving the Terminally Ill and Their Families*. 1979.

National Hospice Organization. Brochure. *Hospice in America*. 1979.

Unpublished Papers

Briggs, J. Maurice. "Family Systems Considerations in Pastoral Supervision." Presentation to CPE Supervisory Staff, North Carolina Baptist Hospitals, Inc., School of Pastoral Care, Winston-Salem, NC (February 1988). Cited by permission.

Hasty, Mary Catherine. "Women's Issues in Pastoral Supervision." Presentation to CPE Supervisory Staff, North Carolina Baptist Hospitals, Inc., School of Pastoral Care, Winston-Salem, NC (Fall 1987). Cited by permission.

Suggested Readings

Colgrove, Melba, Bloomfield, Harold, and McWilliams, Peter. *How to Survive the Loss of a Love*. Allen Park, MI: Leo Press. Eleventh printing, 1981.

Lewis, C. S. *A Grief Observed*. London: Faber and Faber, 1961.

Lindemann, Erich. *Beyond Grief*. New York and London: Jason Aronson, 1979.

Rando, Therese A. *Grief, Dying, and Death: Clinical Interventions for Caregivers*. Champaign, IL: Research Press Company, 1984.

Rando, Therese A., Ed. *Parental Loss of a Child*. Champaign, IL: Research Press Company, 1986.

Reed, Elizabeth Liggett. *Helping Children with the Mystery of Death*. Nashville, TN: Abingdon Press, 1970.

Tolstoy, Leo. *The Death of Ivan Ilyich and Other Stories*. London: Oxford University Press, 1971.

Vanauken, Sheldon. *A Severe Mercy*. New York: Harper & Row, Publishers, 1977.

Wass, Hanelore, and Corr, Charles A. *Childhood and Death*. Washington, DC: Hemisphere Publishing Corporation, A subsidiary of Harper & Row, Publishers, Inc., 1984.

Webb, Nancy Boyd, DSW. *Helping Bereaved Children: A Handbook for Practitioners*. New York and London: The Guilford Press, 1993.

Index

Order Your Own Copy of
This Important Book for Your Personal Library!

DYING, GRIEVING, FAITH, AND FAMILY
A Pastoral Care Approach

_____ in hardbound at $39.95 (ISBN: 0-7890-0262-0)

_____ in softbound at $19.95 (ISBN: 0-7890-0263-9)

COST OF BOOKS_____

OUTSIDE USA/CANADA/
MEXICO: ADD 20%_____

POSTAGE & HANDLING_____
(US: $3.00 for first book & $1.25
for each additional book)
Outside US: $4.75 for first book
& $1.75 for each additional book)

SUBTOTAL_____

IN CANADA: ADD 7% GST_____

STATE TAX_____
(NY, OH & MN residents, please
add appropriate local sales tax)

FINAL TOTAL_____
(If paying in Canadian funds,
convert using the current
exchange rate. UNESCO
coupons welcome.)

☐ **BILL ME LATER:** ($5 service charge will be added)
(Bill-me option is good on US/Canada/Mexico orders only;
not good to jobbers, wholesalers, or subscription agencies.)

☐ Check here if billing address is different from
shipping address and attach purchase order and
billing address information.

Signature_____

☐ **PAYMENT ENCLOSED: $**_____

☐ **PLEASE CHARGE TO MY CREDIT CARD.**

☐ Visa ☐ MasterCard ☐ AmEx ☐ Discover
☐ Diner's Club
Account # _____

Exp. Date _____

Signature _____

Prices in US dollars and subject to change without notice.

NAME _____

INSTITUTION _____

ADDRESS _____

CITY _____

STATE/ZIP _____

COUNTRY _____ COUNTY (NY residents only) _____

TEL _____ FAX _____

E-MAIL_____
May we use your e-mail address for confirmations and other types of information? ☐ Yes ☐ No

Order From Your Local Bookstore or Directly From
The Haworth Press, Inc.
10 Alice Street, Binghamton, New York 13904-1580 • USA
TELEPHONE: 1-800-HAWORTH (1-800-429-6784) / Outside US/Canada: (607) 722-5857
FAX: 1-800-895-0582 / Outside US/Canada: (607) 772-6362
E-mail: getinfo@haworth.com
PLEASE PHOTOCOPY THIS FORM FOR YOUR PERSONAL USE.

BOF96